THE WORST
KIND OF PEOPLE

How to identify and avoid
"energy vampires"

by Roland Kriewaldt

Aurora Sky Publishing
www.AuroraSkyPublishing.com

*I dedicate this book to
everyone who has been the victim
of another's selfish impulses.*

First Paperback Edition
Copyright © 2022 by Roland Kriewaldt

Published globally by
Aurora Sky Publishing

Ordering Info: www.AuroraSkyPublishing.com
Author's website: www.RolandK.ca

All rights reserved. No part of this book may be copied without the expressed written permission of the author. However, short excerpts may be quoted in print or electronic media for the sole purpose of review or promotion.

ISBN *978-0-9686823-7-1*

Cover / Interior Design / Typesetting: Roland Kriewaldt.
(This book uses a hybrid UK/US English spelling because...)

CONTENTS

Preface		iv
Introduction		v
Chapter 1	What is an Energy Vampire?	1
Chapter 2	A History of the Vampire Legend	7
Chapter 3	The Defeaters	15
	The Hypocritic	17
	The Preemptive Striker	19
	The Rabid Reformer	21
	The Wounded Attacker	23
Chapter 4	The Depleters	25
	The Hammerhead	27
	The Joy Killer	29
	Mister Helpless	31
	The Poor Rich Man	33
	The Underwhelming Over-Talker	36
Chapter 5	The Deniers	37
	The Always Offended	39
	The Ill Informer	42
	The Illegal Dumper	43
	The Minimizer	46
	The Selfish Sleeper	48
	The Sunshine Messenger	49
Chapter 6	The Deceivers	51
	The Celebrity Tapeworm	53
	The Crooked Crusader	55
	Dr. Death Defier	56
	The False Profit	57
	The Fame Facilitator	59
	The Gaslight Girl	61
	The Hungry Shopper	62
	Mister Quick And Easy	63
	The Nonsense Seer	66
	The Sexual Decoy	67
Chapter 7	A Word About Victimhood	71
Index		77
About the author:		78

Preface

I don't have kids, but if I did, I would want them to know three crucial pieces of information before entering the adult world:

1) That pornography is not an accurate representation of sexuality.
2) That religion is not an accurate representation of spirituality and,
3) That most of the people who will take advantage of us are not an accurate representation of themselves — they are impostors.

Case in point, history's most notorious arch-villain, Adolf Hitler. Who could have foreseen him sending children into battle in his last desperate bid to cling to power? Or that the German people would let him get away with such insanity by masquerading as their savior? Yet even after leaving their country in ruins, many still adored him.

Although illogical, such devotion stems from our desire to believe in illusions, including the moral supremacy of our leaders, who typically prove our assumptions woefully misguided in hindsight.

As citizens, we often fail to realize that those seeking a leadership role are not always driven by a love for humanity, but a selfish urge to control us so that they can do as they please. In *Clearing a Path to Joy*, I defined this as an aspect of "bio-psychology" and would recommend this book as a guide for avoiding the kind of cultish *mental empires* that seduce us into glorifying vain sociopaths with no interest in helping anyone but themselves. Surely we can all name a few such people.

As for my ambitions, I could have taken an easier route by authoring a picture book of kittens or a cookbook for chocolate lovers. However, my path appears predestined in that I was already getting in trouble with authority figures as a child in Germany when I stood up in front of my Kindergarten class to debate the existence of God with four Catholic nuns there to indoctrinate us into their way of thinking.

As with all my work, I want to expose the illusions of our world so that you or your children will no longer be misled or abused by others. And I do this in the belief that it will improve life *for all of us*.

Roland Kriewaldt — Toronto, Canada.

Introduction

A word of caution — some parts of this book may be disturbing to more sensitive readers. We can blame our survival instinct for this reaction in that it urges us to avoid suffering in any form, including being afraid of suffering itself. In fact, just thinking about distressing matters can cause us to feel compelled to flee courtesy of our *fight or flight* response. For example, we may avoid pondering our imminent death or if the person we trust is betraying us because such fearful thoughts can make us feel vulnerable and insecure rather than strong and confident — which is the way we prefer our thinking to be.

However, we also cannot improve our lives by avoiding the obstacles to our improvement. For instance, we cannot increase our joy in life by ignoring the cause of our unhappiness — nor can we correct lingering social injustices by ignoring their negative impact upon our societies.

Instead, we must allow ourselves to enter this land of shadows and use our righteous anger as the motivation to protect ourselves and our world from being victimized by remorseless human predators.

Ultimately, this book will help increase our social awareness so that we are better protected against those who want to weaken our powers of self-determination or the freedoms of self-expression upon which our joy depends. As such, we owe it to ourselves and each other to give more attention to what we otherwise may not want to think about and perhaps avoid discussing altogether — namely, the darker side of life.

To counter this impulse, let us realize that cowardice is not our fear of doing what is necessary, but our allowing that fear to rule over us in such a way that we refuse to do anything to help ourselves.

And sadly, those who best understand this state of inner conflict are the energy vampires themselves who use our fear to their advantage.

In this book, you will be introduced to four categories of *energy vampires* — the kind of people who want to manipulate us for their own selfish ends. Within each category, various energy vampire types are profiled and their traits and motivations explored.

Among the energy vampire types listed, some are relatively harmless, being more an annoyance than a genuine threat. Yet other types can be highly aggressive and dangerous to all who cross their path, giving us all the more reason to learn how to identify and avoid such people. We may also find both passive and aggressive types under one category if they share a common objective, such as *defeating* our resolve to act.

As you read this book, you may also see aspects of yourself reflected within the character profiles of certain energy vampires. This is because we all have the capacity to behave in harmful ways towards others if we allow our inherent selfishness to prevail within relationships.

This sense of familiarity with the worst of humanity may not come as a pleasant realization, yet it can offer us an opportunity to reevaluate and become more self-aware of how we ourselves treat others.

Ultimately, in gaining greater awareness of social manipulators, we can better protect both our own paths to future joy as well as those of others who may not realize that they have fallen victim to the charms of one of the many types of energy vampires lurking in our midst.

CHAPTER 1
What is an Energy Vampire?

Vampires do not exist, at least not the kind depicted in horror films. And yet, our encounters with people who leave us feeling physically or emotionally drained may tempt us to believe otherwise. Instead, it is likely that we have been in the presence of an energy vampire; a kind of human predator who purposely steals the energy of others.

This energy depletion can take many forms, from drawing on our time, money or physical labor to draining us of self-esteem until we become a submissive slave to their every whim. In that state, we may begin to feel utterly hopeless, spiritually vacant and even lose our will to live.

It is for these reasons and more that we must learn to identify and defend against those selfish social manipulators identified herein, lest they keep feeding upon our lives until we are bled dry.

However, escaping the clutches of an energy vampire is not always easy. After all, sometimes that predator may be a member of our family or a trusted friend who is taking unfair advantage of us. They may also be someone in a position of great power or authority whose parasitical abuses we cannot escape nor defend against if their selfish feasting is enabled by a brutal police or paramilitary force. In this category, we find entire nations being held hostage by crazed dictators or cult-like ideologues similar to what was experienced in World War II courtesy of the Nazis, or in South Africa during Apartheid when an overtly white supremacist government kept black Africans politically weak and economically poor.

As such, the presence of energy vampires and their value systems can pose a serious threat not only to our individual pursuits of happiness, but also to the future survival of our planet when led by those having selfish ambitions to conquer our world — whether through genocide, targeted habitat destruction (as when Europeans decimated buffalo herds to starve out North American indigenous tribes) and the most common method, which is to monopolize all resources, from money to land and water, in order to turn us into dependent slaves.

Sadly, much of our human history is defined by selfish activity of this kind and it continues today as entire nations are being defeated and depleted of energy by way of military warfare, economic slavery, covert political interference by intelligence agencies or business cartels, and the equally covert or even legalized bribing of government officials to make legislative decisions that serve only their own best interests.

And unlike the lore of the vampire, such horror stories are true.

A Word About Prejudice

Knowing what awaits us, the obvious question becomes: *what can we do to keep these energy vampires from feasting upon our energy?*

But before we attempt to answer that question, let us first address a common human folly, which is the thoughtless tendency to demonize others just for disagreeing with our point of view. By exhibiting this kind of a reflexive mental prejudice, we ourselves risk becoming an energy vampire in the lives of others by demanding that they agree with us or suffer our wrath, be it verbally, physically or otherwise.

This attitude also makes it more difficult to be objective when facing unpleasant truths in regard to ourselves. Therefore, it is best that we approach the topic of energy vampires with an open mind and not a self-serving attitude wherein we only attribute bad behavior to those opposing our own definition of "the greater good." After all, we train soldiers to think in such an adversarial way so they can feel justified in killing "the enemy" — including innocent civilians living on the land destined for exploitation by foreign leaders. But we have yet to create the kind of world that will allow us all to live in peace and prosperity by promoting pathological selfishness as a moral philosophy. Instead, it only serves to make *the worst kind of people* even stronger.

In other words, we must be vigilant against our own tendency to act like an energy vampire in the lives of others. In this way, we can avoid victimizing otherwise kind-hearted people with differing views that may even be more enlightened than ours. It will also give us a better chance of living in a world that is fair and balanced in everyone's favor. And ironically, this also answers in part the question of *what can we do about energy vampires?* Quite simply, we must find ways to bring about a greater state of social balance on a global scale so that we no longer live in a world divided into selfish have-lots and ailing have-nots.

In fact, by simply paying attention to and curbing our selfish actions towards others, we can heal many of our world's most lingering social and political problems related to the seeking of power and status.

Yet this is also wishful thinking in part because some people are just not mentally equipped for peaceful social interaction, including those sociopaths who are emotionally unaffected by the harm they can do to others. As a result, we may have to consider more drastic measures or acts of courage to defend against those unwilling to reign in their destructive behavior — or take responsibility for it.

For example, how could ordinary citizens defend against an Adolf Hitler-type dictator who restructures our entire society, from its police and military forces to our ideology and voting rights, to facilitate his abuses of power against us? Yet we cannot even begin to answer such difficult questions if we naively envision our abusers to be our saviors — a mental lapse in judgment that continues to plague us today.

And that is where this book comes in. It can help us to determine if those in whom we trust are truly trustworthy, or just another selfish glutton intent on helping themselves to the lion's share of social power, privilege and prestige at our expense.

What Do Energy Vampires Look Like?

Unlike in the movies, there is no way to identify an energy vampire by how they look. In fact, some will purposely disguise themselves to appear as a person we can trust — be it a priest, police officer, or a high ranking politician flashing a counterfeit smile for the cameras.

This also reveals a problematic side-effect of movies, media and folk story-telling in that we may become prejudiced as to how a dangerous person should appear — perhaps with a hideous scar, rotting teeth or a distinct clothing style to alert us of their presence. As a result, many of us have come to fear phantoms born of our imagination or popular culture, such as those demons warned about by religion. Yet real-life evil-doers can be lurking anywhere in our midst, including in churches or synagogues. Ironically, this can create situations wherein those same evil-doers warn us not to engage with genuinely "good" people so that we can be held as mentally hostages under the influence of their lies. And if we are raised to see our world as they command, then we may go through life oblivious of our being victimized by energy vampires claiming to be the moral leaders or political architects of our future.

Just as hunters use camouflage, so do energy vampires often cloak themselves in the attire and language of their intended victims. The scam artist who wants to steal your life savings, for instance, will often dress like someone who is too wealthy to resort to low level financial crimes, whereas a pedophile may cloak himself in the guise of a school teacher, scout leader or religious cleric to gain access to children.

This forces us to confront the reality that there will be times when a truly *bad* person appears to be one of the *good* people so that we might be lulled into a false sense of security before they strike to claim their next victim — whether ourselves or one of our children.

As such a major vulnerability in dealing with energy vampires is how we are culturally *socialized* to think. This can cause us to leave our guard down at the worst of times or even accept systemic abuse or outright crimes against humanity as a normal part of life. In that regard, we need only consider the continued plight of women under the influence of any male-dominated "patriarchal" society.

The Folly of False Assumptions

What we will find throughout our world is that once our thinking is compromised by indoctrination to any belief system, it can impede our ability to see others as they truly are. Instead, we may see them as we have been trained to see them.

For instance, devoutly religious parents may not allow themselves to belief that their religious leader could be a child molester or financial grifter. And such programmed ignorance is the leverage that allows energy vampires of many kinds to carry out their shameless crimes undetected in our midst.

However, we also cannot go through life assuming that everyone is guilty until proven innocent, otherwise societies would fail due to our widespread distrust of others. Instead, we tend to direct prejudice in predictable ways that betray a deeper underlying motive, which is our inherent desire for power and status. As such, we tend to favor the wealthy while denigrating the poor; a common feature of all societies that have class and caste-based systems. The same self-serving motive is also evident in racism, wherein we judge those of other races inferior to our own kind. One ironic outcome of such status seeking is that it causes many light skinned Africans to judge darker skinned Africans as inferior — whereas both are seen as inferior by white supremacists in all countries. And so we see that it is more a mental game we play rather than something having a foundation in truth or reality.

Yet the significance of such status-seeking prejudice is that energy vampires can often become leaders of nations by playing up this desire among citizens to feel above others in some way. And so, for those who supported Hitler, it was partly due to their wanting to feel "better than" people of other creeds or nationalities that would allow this madman to lead them into a disastrous and humiliating war.

As a result, we are all susceptible to making false assumptions and unfair judgments about others based on how we think or have been conditioned to think, whether by our parents, teachers, government leaders, or even the commercial media. Taking all of this into account, we therefore require some means to identify genuine Energy Vampires that is not discolored by our private fears, ambitions or prejudices.

In that regard, one reliable way to identify an energy vampire or any kind of social predator is to observe their interactions with others. If they are always manipulating and treating others with the same selfish disregard, then they may well be one of the many energy vampire types of whom we will learn in this book.

As for what we can do to protect ourselves against their threat, our best defense is to learn to identity such people and their behaviors so that we can avoid them or plan some appropriate strategy to prevent them from stealing any more of our valuable life energy.

In many cases, such a person may pose no genuine threat and only be a nuisance. For example, they may try to constantly monopolize our attention, leaving us no time to give attention to anyone else, including ourselves. In such cases, that person may also be too self-absorbed in catering to their own selfish needs to notice or feel concerned about how their behavior is adversely affecting others. The difficult part, of course, is having to summon the courage to speak up or walk away.

At other times, we may find ourselves confronted by a remorseless human predator who is purposely seeking to victimize those who are young, weak, naïve or overly-trusting of strangers. In this case, we must be willing to take a more active role to rid ourselves of their threat to our society.

However, whatever response you choose is at your discretion, given that it may require leaving that person behind or fighting back legally or even physically to overcome their tyranny over your existence.

That said, in no way does this book condone violence or revenge as a solution for dealing with energy vampires. Its purpose is to teach you how to better protect yourself by identifying the kind of people who take unfair advantage of others without regard for their happiness or future well-being. And obviously, they must be stopped.

CHAPTER 2
A History of the Vampire Legend

Before we meet our human energy vampires, it may be helpful to first understand how they earned their name.

This chapter is not required reading but offers a useful and revealing overview of why the metaphor "vampire" is used to describe those who prey upon others for selfish gain. And if you already understand the origin of the term, you may still find this chapter amusing as a mental stroll down one of the darker lanes of human history where fact from fiction is not so easily discernible. Otherwise, for those less patient, you can jump ahead to the next chapter where the profiles begin.

...

The idea of a vampire in human form entered our popular culture in 1897, when author Bram Stoker released his epic novel, Dracula. Since that time, the traits of his imaginative character have been generously amended by way of films and offshoot novels inspired by the original. And, as author Anne Rice discovered in writing her best-selling novels, vampires also offer a lucrative theme through which to address the more horrifying aspects of human behavior without having to point a finger directly at the guilty party.

But long before Bram Stoker's fictitious Count Dracula was to fill our minds with a host of new horrors, there existed a true vampire in the form of a small tropical bat found in South and Central America.

Let us therefore consider how the behavior of the vampire bat took hold of our collective imagination to create that legendary neck-sucker condemned to walk the earth in an eternal quest for blood.

The Real Vampire

The vampire bat is not unlike a blood-sucking insect in that it must also drink the blood of its host to survive. However, it does not drink with its fangs but uses its tongue instead to lap up droplets of blood exiting from a puncture wound made by its sharp teeth. And unlike the mythical vampire, in the aftermath of such a bite, the host animal does not transform into a night-dwelling bloodsucker but instead carries on living a normal life.

There is, however, one exception, which is when that vampire bat has rabies. In that case, the host animal can slowly die from a wasting brain disease that causes a variety of unsettling symptoms. These range from refusing to drink and wandering aimlessly in a stupor to attacking and biting other animals or people, which is how that fatal disease can be transferred from one warm-blooded host to another via the saliva.

As we would expect, anyone witnessing this kind of a transformation in the behavior of a farm animal or fellow human being would feel quite distressed. More importantly, they would do whatever they could to avoid being bitten by a vampire bat and suffer such a dreadful end.

Although based on speculation, we can begin to theorize how garlic may have gained its reputation for warding off vampires.

As we know, garlic emits a powerful odor from the body and breath when eaten and proves highly effective in keeping people from getting too close to us. Containing high levels of sulfur compounds, it has also been used as an antibacterial agent to fight infections. In short, it may not smell very appealing on our breath, but it has its benefits.

Using our creative imagination, we can speculate that some parents may even have used garlic's offensive odor to protect their virginal daughters from the lusty advances of adolescent boys in the village. And in regions where vampire bats exist, perhaps people covered their skin or cow's hide with garlic hoping to confuse a hungry vampire bat's sense of smell as it searched for warm-blooded prey. Admittedly, there is no proof that garlic can repel either vampires bats or lusty adolescent boys. But if horse urine is being used in women's perfume to attract men, then anything seems possible where folk remedies are concerned.

While offered with a touch of humor, garlic does have a long history of being useful, including in the treatment of bacterial infections. And given our superstitious human nature along with its repellent odor, this may have won garlic its place of honor among the symbolic weaponry used to ward off an attack by Bram Stoker's mythical blood sucker.

The Truth Behind the Vampire Myth

The folk legend of the "werewolf" is worth noting here in that it also involves the victim turning into the animal causing the bite. We might then speculate that such supernatural transformations are metaphors to warn us about the bite of an infected wolf or bat, given that it may lead to our contracting the same disease of our animal attacker.

What we may also notice is how folklore is used to protect us from harm by exaggerating some genuine threat, whether from a dangerous person, animal or force of nature. As such, there may not be a witch in the nearby forest, but there could be sufficient wild animals or human predators lurking there to teach our children not to enter alone as did young Hansel and Gretel at the behest of their scheming parents.

In addition, the lingering potency of the Dracula myth may be due to its combining various truths with traditional superstitions to create a frightfully believable folk tale. Among those truths is that every life form must feed on the energy of another life form to exist. And since energy never dies but only transforms, that hunger is eternal. As such, we are all one form of energy consuming it in others forms to feed our hunger for existence.

This hunger for energy has often led to acts of cannibalism, as when the infamous whaling boat, Essex, was sunk by an angry sperm whale, setting twenty men adrift at sea for weeks. In their dire situation, the man who drew the shortest straw was volunteered to be eaten by the other survivors. Such disturbing truths only give further credibility to the story of a vampire that also hunts human prey for its meals.

Beyond eating our own kind out of sheer desperation, some of our ancestors also engaged in cannibalism as a symbolic dominance ritual to steal the power of their enemies. Such behavior was still prevalent among jungle tribes as Europeans were being introduced to indoor plumbing. As such, this is not ancient human history, but something recent that may still be occurring in parts of our world.

The significance of such rituals is in the widely held belief that by eating the flesh of our enemies, we can consume their "life essence." Given that we humans tend to think more symbolically, this has also led to our eating tigers and other apex predators in a naïve attempt to steal their vitality or mental cunning. This is also why the rhinoceros population has been decimated due to human males who believe that eating a rhinoceros horn will give them a larger, firmer erection.

As a result of such symbolic thinking, many animal species have now disappeared or become endangered from overkill. Hence, it proves that symbolic thinking is not only an ancient form of interacting with our world, but can also define our cultural attitudes and behavior — from worshipping the sun to using money as a symbol for social power. But even beyond this, it explains why some psychopathic killers will eat the flesh of their victims in a ritualized attempt to *steal* their life energy.

The symbology of blood is also well-established as the essence of life, for when it stops flowing, we will die. As a result, the drinking of blood represents a powerful metaphor exploited by the Dracula myth as the reason for this creature's incessant hunting for new blood donors, who are then afflicted by that same disease — a quasi-rabies transformation that causes the affected victim to then also feast upon human beings.

The point here is that the myth of Dracula becomes more plausible when supported by aspects of human life that ring true, not the least of which is our lengthy history of eating our own kind for purposes of food and ritual sacrifice. There is also the rabies transfer aspect and our own endless quest for the energy of others, which is the story of life.

Beyond this, Dracula's unconscionable behavior also rings truer in the reader's mind knowing that blood-lusting psychopaths such as *Jack the Ripper* have always lurked in our midst. The only difference is that our own night-prowling villain sleeps in a coffin between meals.

The Legendary Count Drakulya

Bram Stoker's own vampire, Count Dracula, was inspired in part by the colorful life of Vlad Drakulya (aka Vlad Tepes). He was the prince of Walachia and apparently also a sadistic psychopath who terrorized the lives of many during his lifetime, between 1428-1477.

Historically, Vlad was depicted as a ruthless tyrant by his surviving enemies, yet he was also seen as a hero by those Romanians whose lives he defended against hostile Saxon invaders and religious mercenaries. His name, reputation and storybook homeland setting were the ideal artistic fodder for the Irish author to write his Gothic horror novel in 1897, which drew upon the prince's reputation as "Vlad, the Impaler" to create a truly fiendish human monster to frightfully entertain us.

Vlad's brutal piercings of human beings foreshadows why vampires were later said only to die by being *impaled* in their hearts.

Since his original creation, our fictional Dracula has been further bestowed with superhuman traits and some odd weaknesses, including his repulsion for garlic cloves and Christian religious symbols.

In regard to the latter, adding the crucifix as a weapon to ward off vampire attacks was an act of religious propaganda to suggest that the Catholic Church has the power to subdue every manner of evil. It also demonstrates our historical reliance on superstition wherein we wield physical objects in attempting to gain some control over our lives in an uncertain world. Here, where our frail bodies offer no defense against legitimate predators, we often need a little extra-celestial intervention to make it through the day. As such, this also explains our long history of buying magic "snake oil" potions and lucky charms to give ourselves a false sense of power over the Gods and demons of religion, the forces of nature, or just the fickle hand of fate. And so we can understand why we might also reach for various objects or ceremonial rituals to soothe our fears once the sun goes down and the vampires come out.

Bram's Stoker's Dracula lived an eternal life, a claim that is also easy to accept given how many of us believe in an afterlife. In addition, he also feared and avoided sunlight — clearly a metaphor for the gaining of wisdom, whether through religious indoctrination or a much longer and solitary inward journey of introspection toward self-knowledge.

Dracula's allergy to sunlight also makes the story more believable in that we would not expect a remorseless killer to care about morality or virtue in satisfying his insatiable bloodlust. That urge also makes an apt metaphor for the insatiable greed that has long plagued our world at the hands of various human predators. Their savage appetite for money and power further makes Count Dracula's own remorseless lust for blood all the more believable.

From Fangs to Foul Play

We can now make this connection between a mythical bloodsucking human vampire — a form of cultural entertainment — and the reality of there truly existing "energy vampires" in human form who will drain us of everything we have in life to feed their own insatiable appetites.

The nature of that appetite may vary from person to person, yet most have a need to fill some lingering void in their lives, be it emotional, economic, sexual or otherwise. In short, there is something missing in their existence that they hope to regain by victimizing others. And so they may attempt to assert their dominance over a weaker person to prove their own power, or make us the host to their parasitic lifestyle.

This is also why we must be extremely cautious when engaging with others on social media for the purpose of having our dreams fulfilled. All too often, we may be tempted into the lair of some energy vampire who will promise us anything to lure us deeper into their online trap.

Here, we may encounter images of attractive young women posing in bikinis as they attempt to trick lonely men into becoming hosts to their parasitic demands for money or attention. Meanwhile, others will present themselves as experts in the fields of health or finance to trick us into sending them our money. And sadly, many of us do.

While their antics represent a low-level threat in the realm of human predators, it is their type of behavior that has inspired this metaphoric association between Bram Stoker's fiendish night-prowler and those kinds of people who will mercilessly feed upon others without any sign of having either a guilty conscience or feelings of remorse.

In their own quest to consume our energy as advertising time, the news media will parade the worst of these human predators before us in the form of serial killers, rapists and pedophiles. Yet we must always keep in mind that those kinds of people do not grow from spores in some castle dungeon but are born and raised in the societies where the rest of us are hoping to live a happy and prosperous life. In short, such people have always been in our midst throughout human history. And all too often, we cannot detect their presence until it is too late.

As such, we must all learn to identify energy vampires so that we can avoid becoming the victim of their selfish exploits, whether in context of a parasitic marriage, friendship, our membership in some religious or political organization, a business partnership or as a prospect in any "Get Rich Quick" investment scheme meant to make us only poorer.

Introducing the Energy Vampires.

In the chapters that follow, you will be introduced to four categories of energy vampires, each with its own distinct section.

Within each section is an introduction to describe that particular energy vampire type; the motives for their behavior; a list of methods they might employ to manipulate us; some of their weaknesses and vulnerabilities if we choose to fight back against them, and also their negative impact on various kinds of relationships.

After reading this introduction, you will be shown the profiles for various energy vampire types listed under that category based on some common trait as defined for that category.

In the final chapter, you will also find some additional information and helpful advice for avoiding energy vampires of various kinds. This is an important section that should not be ignored by anyone who believe themselves to be the victim of this kind of human predation.

And now, it's time to meet our energy vampires.

CHAPTER 3
The Defeaters

CATEGORY DESCRIPTION:
The Defeater seeks to control others using various mental and physical forms of aggression to intimidate their victims into submission.

UNDERLYING MOTIVES:
The Defeater wants to control others to gain privileged access to social advantages or material resources ranging from preferred sexual access and money to political influence and leadership of a nation.

METHODS OF MANIPULATION:
The Defeater may use a variety of tactics to "defeat" us. These include the use of belittling insults, theatrical displays of anger, loud aggressive yelling, physical intimidation, kicking, punching, restraint, captivity, torture, murder and full scale military warfare to defeat anyone who resists being controlled by this selfish oppressor.

WEAKNESSES AND VULNERABILITIES:
The Defeater fears losing their power over those who they exploit to serve their own selfish ends.

NEGATIVE IMPACT ON RELATIONSHIPS:
The Defeater wants controlling interest in any relationship or dealing with others. To gain such an advantage, they will try to defeat us rather than negotiate a fair settlement. As the recipient of their ill treatment, we can expect little in return beyond a life of misery in feeling trapped,

hopeless, afraid and hateful toward our oppressor, who has little regard for how their pathological selfishness is affecting the lives of others.

WHO ARE THE DEFEATERS?

A defeater is someone who attempts to gain absolute control over our lives to gain greater control over their own. Their methods are to defeat us in body, mind or spirit until we surrender to their demands. This will result in a master-to-slave kind of relationship wherein we are treated as an appendage of their will or an object in their possession. In this way, we live as though we do not matter while our needs and wants are ignored by an oppressor too busy with tending to their own.

Ironically, selfish tyrants such as these often see themselves as heroic leaders simply doing what is "best" for those they exploit and abuse. In their minds, they may see their victims as helpless children or herds of mindless human cattle. This attitude also allows them to feel justified in maintaining their oppressive control over others by any means, be it mental, physical, social, economic or spiritual warfare.

Yet despite their declarations of altruism or goodwill in dominating others, their actions speak for themselves in denying us our freedom to express ourselves or become the authentic person we were born to be. Instead, we may live in constant state of fear of being punished or injured for expressing ourselves in some "wrong" way that may offend this ill-minded dictator who is holding our life hostage and declaring themselves our lord and master.

As anyone in such an oppressive relationship knows, we must live as impostors, obediently nodding our heads and pretending to agree with anything that this tyrant says, even when we strongly disagree.

As with all energy vampires described in this book, the Defeaters are categorized by the methods they use to achieve their selfish aims. Let us now consider those types found within the *defeater* category.

The Hypocritic

Profile Overview:
The Hypocritic is a loud, aggressive tyrant who is ultimately exposed for moral failings or character flaws that far exceed those of the people they condemn. In the meantime, they can inflict great harm within our homes or communities, psychologically and otherwise, if we fall under the spell of this vainglorious poser with so much to hide.

The behavior of a Hypocritic may be driven by several motives, the obvious being to compete for social status or glory by making everyone else seem inferior. Also, by posing as a morally or ideologically superior individual, they can exploit those looking for someone to guide them. The Hypocritic will therefore often take a leadership role in groups by masquerading as someone of higher virtue and integrity, at least until their inevitable fall from grace in being exposed as a fraud.

A further motive finds the Hypocritic harshly criticizing others as a smokescreen to distract from their own shortcomings. For example, a man who fails to succeed in life may criticize the failures of other men to deflect criticism away from himself. Likewise, politicians often draw negative attention toward their opponents while seeming oblivious of their own unsavory traits and self-serving behaviors.

Hypocritics are "defeaters" in that they use their words as weapons to keep others beneath them in stature. As a flawed individual who is merely pretending to be perfect, they are also not known for confessing their crimes, even if caught in the act of breaking those very rules and moral codes for which they condemn others. And if their goal is to build a cultish empire of servile followers, then they will often resort to drastic measures to protect their pretentious pedestals of power.

Familiar Examples:
Having already failed the Aryan look-alike contest, Adolf Hitler, in an epic act of hypocritical projection, claimed the Jews were trying to rule the world as he fought to rule it himself. Further examples include the

many religious leaders who expound the virtues of poverty for others while living a life of opulent luxury in some upscale gated community.

We may also find the Hypocritic inside our homes as a domineering parent who demands that others live up to standards of excellence that they have yet to achieve. Using verbal abuse and threats, they keep us focussed on serving only their own best interests, not ours.

Energy Losses Incurred:
Given that our eyes look outward, it is easier to see what everyone else is doing wrong. This is why we can all succumb to bouts of hypocrisy, not out of sinister intent, but in failing to be objective in our dealings with others. In stark contrast, the Hypocritic is a sociopath who is fully aware of their two-faced nature and shows only that face which gives them the winning advantage over others.

As a tragic example of this, an American televangelist famous for his condemnation of homosexuals was later exposed as being one himself. In the meantime, his messages of self-loathing reached many millions of viewers, perhaps leading some to suicide. As another "man of god" enjoying an excessively opulent lifestyle, he used his platform to incite hatred for those who had summoned the courage to embrace their own inner truth so as not to live as hypocrites themselves.

The Hypocritic is the destroyer of families and nations for they can undermine our self-esteem and even cause violent social uprisings. As such, we must expose them as soon as their actions betray their words and publicly confront them for others to see who they truly are. In the meantime, they may live a joyless life of denial in always having to hide from the truth. A personal crisis may break their resolve, yet most will desperately cling to their pretense of superiority to protect their hold on power or to justify their often narcissistic sense of entitlement.

We can best protect ourselves and our societies by always exposing Hypocritics as the lying charlatans that they are — no matter how highly placed they may be atop the pyramid of social status and power. And always, we must pay close attention to their contradictory actions, for their words are meant to hide them from our view.

The Preemptive Striker

General Overview:
Whether as children or young adults, we have all had encounters with people who make us feel weak and vulnerable. The Preemptive Striker is such a person, attacking others first as a way to intimidate them into submission. In this way, we are less likely to strike back or challenge them in any future negotiation or debate.

This is also a turning point in any relationship in that, from now on, they can assume their entitlement to any social advantage or privilege in having aroused our fear of retribution should we dare to challenge their right to whatever they want, whenever they want it.

While this kind of bluffing and intimidation behavior is common in the wild among males declaring territorial or sexual dominance, it is entirely out of place in our homes where families must work as a team to ensure one another's mutual well-being. But the Preemptive Striker is a *defeater* having no interest in peaceful compromises. Instead, like an invading army, they seek only the complete surrender of those who oppose them, whether through mental or physical violence.

Such preemptive aggression is not the result of an immediate threat but the attacker's anticipation of a threat. Its purpose is to put us on the defensive so that we will be afraid to strike first. Such behavior can be the symptom of early childhood trauma, a relic of growing up in a patriarchal culture, or the psychological misfirings of an undiagnosed psychopath making their way through life as a social predator.

Attacks typically occur when an aggressor feels vulnerable — which also means that their state of mind may only be a product of their own imagination. They will then attempt to transfer that fear to others by making us feel as vulnerable as they do. Subsequently, the Preemptive Striker also lives in constant fear of losing control over those they force into submission, leading to a joyless life wherein everyone treats them more like an enemy than a welcome friend or family member.

The Preemptive Striker's aggression makes them a threat to intimate relationships or parenting. Yet sexual promiscuity and economics often find such a person at the head of a family household wherein everyone lives as a frightened prisoner under the tyranny of this abusive guard.

As a defeater, the Preemptive Striker desires to win. Yet ultimately they become the loser in their private war against the world as friends and family turn away to protect themselves. And as leaders of a nation, they become the target of the people's wrath for keeping them servile and obedient in a culture of psychological terror and brutal violence.

Familiar Examples:
The Preemptive Striker is that childhood bully who lets everyone know that he rules the schoolyard with his only qualification for leadership being his fists. They are that manipulative employer who makes veiled threats that we will be fired or passed over for a promotion before they demand that we work longer hours for less pay. They are that deeply insecure marriage partner whose jealousy rages out of control; whose probing interrogations of our daily whereabout or actions make us feel like a powerless child forced to answer to an angry parent.

Energy Losses Incurred:
The Preemptive Striker steals our energy by inhibiting our ability to express ourselves in any way that might cause them to feel threatened. This can suppress our personal growth and lead to future failure if we no longer feel any desire to set goals or seek to improve ourselves due to feeling hopelessly trapped in a cage of fear. The same is true of any citizen living under an oppressive political or religious regime.

The Preemptive Striker's selfish nature also makes them behave like a slave owner rather than a relationship partner. As such, they might make constant demands on our time and energy while offering little in return because they interpret *giving* to others as losing to them. For this reason, sharing is not in their nature. However, in another form of preemptive strike, they may put on a show of generosity if they suspect that others are watching them. In doing this, they also hope to defeat the anticipated negative reactions of others to their selfishness.

Energy Vampire Profile

The Rabid Reformer

Profile Overview:
Rarely will we meet a more repentant individual than the "sinner" who has seen the error of their ways. Yet some people exude a competitive aggression in declaring their victory over any personal struggle in their life. Among them is the Rabid Reformer who wields their conquests over adversity as a weapon to set themselves apart from others. Instead of using their stories of struggle to inspire, they turn them into a kind of promotional vehicle for declaring themselves a "winner" over others.

Their behavior is not to be confused with the near fanatical desire of people to prove their commitment to a personal life change. Most are preaching the gospel of their conversion merely to reassure themselves to stay the course. By contrast, the Rabid Reformer uses their victory over adversity as an opportunity to boast and present themselves as being superior to those still struggling to overcome similar challenges. As a result, they exude an air of selfishness because their intention is to win praise and steal our attention rather than help or reassure others.

Familiar Examples:
Like other social primates, humans are status-conscious. This causes our competitive social posturing to establish dominance or prevent the illusion of our superiority from being eroded by our challengers. This is also the underlying cause of human vanity and arrogance. Knowing this, we can better distinguish a Rabid Reformer's more pathological social behavior from that of others.

Many of us will share the joy of a personal victory with our family or friends, not to gain a competitive advantage, but because we know that this will make them happy, too. We can therefore detect a Rabid Reformer by their negative impact upon our emotional state in that they will draw attention to their superiority to make us feel inferior.

For example, they may boast of adopting some new and improved lifestyle in such a way as to imply we are a "loser" for still doing things "the old-fashioned way." Among that list of personal life changes, the Rabid Reformer may boast to us about:

- ☑ Having conquered an addiction to food, alcohol or nicotine in a way that makes us feel ridiculed for still indulging in those habits or addictions.
- ☑ Having discovered some universal "truth" in a way that suggests that we are naïve and gullible for defending our own personal beliefs.
- ☑ Having become a vegan in such a way that we are made to feel like an abuser of animals.
- ☑ Having purchased a new health supplement in a way that makes us feel as though we prefer to remain unhealthy or unwilling to care for ourselves.
- ☑ Having joined a religion or new age cult in a way that makes us want to avoid Heaven altogether, in case we might encounter them there.

Rabid Reformers will even victimize entire cultures to claim the upper hand. In one infamous case, under the pretense of doing "God's work," Christian nuns and missionaries beat, tortured and even killed aboriginal children in Canada in forcing them to give up their "savage" ways of thinking and behaving. Yet with the clarity of hindsight, we now see that these self-proclaimed promoters of God's love were the only ones acting like savages. While this must not prejudice us against religious followers doing useful missionary work, it does alert us to the reality that not everyone claiming to work for God is an angel. In fact, their actions may suggest quite the opposite.

Energy Losses Incurred:
The Rabid Reformer poses a genuine threat to our joy and well-being in that they approach us as an adversary rather than a friend. We are "the enemy" to conquer for the sake of boosting their self-image. Given that we can now anticipate such a negative outcome, we might reply to them that we are happy to hear of their triumph over adversity and that we hope it has made them a far happier and more caring person in the lives of others. At this point, we might casually walk away to let them spend some more time alone with their newfound happiness.

The Wounded Attacker

Profile Overview:

As the name suggests, the wounded attacker is someone who lashes out at others as the result of some prior emotional injury, whether to their self-esteem or feeling of significance. Such a person is often vain and status-conscious, causing them to feel competitively threatened when others achieve greater success or are working to improve themselves. As such, the Wounded Attacker resents our achievements because they act as a painful reminder of their own failures to succeed in life.

To counteract their feelings of inferiority, a Wounded Attacker will often attempt to mentally defeat those who have attained success. But instead of attempting to rise above them in status, they will attempt to pull that person down in some way to below their own level.

In social settings, they may try to assassinate the character of their perceived rivals by searching for flaws in their success or even in their outward appearance. In this way, they gain a false sense of superiority without having to make an effort to actually prove themselves superior on a level playing field where they are likely to suffer a humiliating defeat at the hands of those they choose to ridicule.

Familiar Examples:

The Wounded Attacker is often someone with high aspirations yet a limited potential. In realizing that they cannot rise up or win by their own merit, they set out to pull the true winners down as an alternative means to elevating their own status. Such behavior may be familiar to us from high school, where naturally attractive girls were often openly loathed by every girl yearning for such status and attention. Elsewhere, mental underachievers taunt the intellectually gifted for failing to live up to the shallow standards of the masculine or feminine tribal culture.

When "sore losers" such as this enter adulthood, we may find them working in media as hateful political pundits or acid-tongued critics gleefully denouncing those who have attained genuine success. In this way, they gain popularity for their offering of emotional sanctuary and social redemption to audiences of equally low-esteemed individuals who have likewise chosen envy-fueled hatred over self-improvement.

Known for their competitive hostility, some rise to prominence not for being gifted, but for pulling down those having a gift. We find the same attitude in celebrity gossip culture wherein the envious can revel in the misery of rich and famous people struggling with adversity. By "dishing out the dirt" on the successful, those refusing to reach for their own dreams are made to feel better for never having tried.

Another example is the heckler who yells insults at performers to undermine their confidence. In reality, they are publicly declaring their own emotional wounds in seeing someone get more attention. And so they try to draw the audiences attention toward themselves.

Energy Losses Incurred:
The Wounded Attacker seeks to minimize the victories of others as "illegitimate wins" to excuse their own losses in life. As such, they often accuse a winner of having an unfair advantage even if they succeeded by virtue of having greater strength, skill or talent. In losing a race, for instance, they might blame a leg injury or circumstance beyond their control rather than admit that the winning runner was simply better.

The Wounded Attacker poses a threat to our joy and well-being in that any achievement in our life threatens to overshadow their own. As the child of a vain parent, for instance, we may be denied the attention or praise we deserve from someone who wants to monopolize all the glory for themselves. They may even try to undermine our confidence or enthusiasm for making significant personal progress to ensure that we remain with them in the same lowly predicament.

Ironically, their presence offers us a valuable spiritual lesson in that it reveals the importance of loving ourselves and celebrating our own victories because no one else is obligated to do so. And if we are truly strong in our sense of identity and purpose, then trivial matters such as gaining other people's applause or recognition will have little worth in comparison to our own inner feelings of joy and contentment.

CHAPTER 4
The Depleters

CATEGORY DESCRIPTION:
The Depleter is someone who depletes the energy of others in various forms, including mental, physical and monetary.

UNDERLYING MOTIVES:
The Depleter seeks to avoid changes or life challenges that may lead to their own loss of energy, suffering or feelings of discomfort.

METHODS OF MANIPULATION:
The Depleter controls others by exploiting their feelings of guilt and pity or by emotionally sabotaging their attempts at self-improvement.

WEAKNESSES AND VULNERABILITIES:
The Depleter fears change and the unknown and feels threatened when their sense of mental or physical comfort is challenged or at risk.

NEGATIVE IMPACT ON RELATIONSHIPS:
The Depleter tries to prevent us from making positive life changes or achieving personal goals, which ultimately leads to our feeling hopeless and unhappy in having our enthusiasm for life constantly depleted.

WHO ARE THE DEPLETERS?
The Depleter tries to steal our energy to weaken our resolve. They do this by keeping us from changing our life in a way that could have an adverse affect on their own life circumstances or personal comfort.

Such a person is also typically a spectator of life rather than an active participant or inspirational figure in the lives of others. Instead, they are more a burden to mutual progress by bringing less than their equal share of effort into any relationship. As such, we should not expect them to show enthusiasm for our own attempts to achieve a personally meaningful goal. Instead, they would prefer that we just sat down and stopped making them look bad for failing to have the same initiative.

We must not confuse the Depleter with the chronically ill or those who may otherwise require our constant attendance. Instead, they are incapacitated only by their "No-can-do!" attitude, which they may also encourage us to adopt in order to maintain their lifestyle of inertia.

Such a person may also be too self-obsessed with their own misery to offer others moral support or their own selfless, undivided attention. Instead, they may make constant and continuing demands on our time and energy in a life defined by serving only their own selfish needs.

The Depleter is not an aggressive energy vampire type. Instead, they having a negative controlling influence over our lives by acting like an anchor that is tethered to our ambitions to succeed. In this way, they are better assured that we will remain with them in the safety of that familiar harbor of comfort in which their lives are moored.

As the upcoming profiles reveal, the energy we can potentially lose to a Depleter can take many forms beyond money and material goods. Yet their goal is always the same, in that they will do everything in their power to avoid change, thereby not only sabotaging their own progress toward living a more joyfully contented life, but also everyone else's.

The Hammerhead

Profile Overview:
The Hammerhead is familiar to many of us as someone who is always complaining about the problems they create for themselves, whether out of carelessness or their refusal to take corrective action. The name was inspired by imagining someone holding a hammer and repeatedly hitting themselves on the head with it while complaining of having a headache. Yet the most significant aspect of their behavior is that when we suggest putting the hammer away, they will instead find an excuse to continue holding on to it for just a little while longer — which often turns into years or even their entire lifetime.

The "hammer" is a metaphor for any kind of self-defeating behavior for which the Hammerhead refuses to take personal responsibility or remedial action to correct that behavior.

Familiar Examples:
The Hammerhead can be found as that food addict who is constantly eating while complaining of being overweight, or the alcoholic who is drinking themselves into a state of oblivion each day yet complaining of their deteriorating health or family life. They may also complain of not having the same quality of life as others yet refuse to take steps to improve their life circumstances or chances of succeeding. This is when we begin to realize that the Hammerhead would rather complain than do anything to improve their situation.

Energy Losses Incurred:
The Hammerhead engages in a life of contradictory behavior wherein they intentionally hurt themselves while complaining about their pain. This betrays their true intentions, which is to use their complaining as the emotional bait to draw out sympathy and attention from others.

Often, that person is simply trying to manipulate us by appealing to our innate sense of humanity — our urge to help others in need. In this way, we may also waste valuable time, energy and resources in helping someone who may no want their problems solved because they draw to them the kind of attention they may not have gotten as a child from their parents or community.

Such people are often emotionally needy, turning them into energy vampires who drain the lives of others for their own selfish purposes. As such, they also tend to show little regard for how their behavior is affecting those upon whose time and energy they constantly feed.

As the victim of those who suffer from this kind of victim mentality, we cannot be blamed for doing what comes naturally, which is to care. Most group animals show the same response if their competitive fears are not getting in the way. After all, it is only logical to show concern for the well-being of others because our own well-being often depends on it. As a result, many of us will help those who are injured or in need; an innate empathy response that has helped human societies to survive by giving us the urge to protect one another from harm.

Unfortunately, the Hammerhead is often oblivious or too selfish to care how their demands impact others and waste their time. Instead, they use our sympathetic responses to satisfy their emotional craving for attention or undeserved compliments and reassurances. As such, our best defense is to limit our exposure to such people and just offer them the tools to help themselves. In this way, we can avoid being drawn into their self-obsessed victimhood dramas. However, the one tool we cannot provide them with is the motivation to succeed.

It can be difficult for a helpful person not to help others. Yet we also cannot help anyone who does not want to help themselves. Nor can we help those who are truly in need if someone else is monopolizing our time in an effort to relive the emotional comfort of being an infant.

We must be especially careful to recognize when the Hammerhead's habitual cries for help are beginning to deplete our own enthusiasm for life or otherwise cause us to not give ourselves the proper attention we need. After all, if helping them is causing us to disregard ourselves, then we may eventually enter a state of energy depletion wherein we can no longer help anyone, including ourselves.

Energy Vampire Profile

The Joy Killer

Profile Overview:

The Joy Killer is a cynical pessimist; a habitual disenchanter who may resent our joy and try to make us feel as miserable as they do. To do so, they will attempt to undermine our hope for the future or any feelings of trust and confidence we have in our ability to succeed.

We will know such a person by how they make us feel; their presence in any room feels like an emotional anvil weighing us down. They seem offended by the sight or sound of anyone having a buoyant spirit or positive outlook on life. As such, if our spiritual cup is noticeably full, they will try to push us off balance emotionally so that our enthusiasm for life will spill out and leave us without hope. This subverting of our positive outlook on life is what makes them an energy vampire.

Familiar Examples:

The Joy Killer can be identified by their relentless attitude of futility and the cynical way in which they speak of their prospects for life in the future. In justifying their morbid perspective, they must prove that our own quest for joy is a worthless cause. As part of their thesis, they may tell us that happiness is merely a byproduct of chemical reactions within our mechanized brains, or that we are in denial of "reality" in making plans for a future deemed meaningless by our inevitable death from old age or disease. In their value system, living is a waste of time.

Ironically, like the rest of us, they must also stimulate their emotions to feel alive. However, the Joy Killer typically relies on "schadenfreude" to get their thrills as they revel with exaggerated glee in the unexpected downfall or failure of others. Ironically, this further proves their theory about the futility of setting worthwhile goals to improve the quality of our life, especially from a spiritual perspective. In this way they can gloat over how clever they are to not succumb to such idle temptations as cloud the judgments and mental perceptions of everyone else. This also suggests a socially-competitive, status-seeking component to their dismissal of others by implying their own intellectual superiority.

Energy Losses Incurred:
The Joy Killer is known to use derogatory and belittling criticism as a means to keep others down, which can undermine the self-confidence of those who believe that this doomsayer is an authority figure with a great deal of experience in seeking a life of joy. In reality, it appears that they have given up that quest, or may never even have made the effort to take the first courageous step forward in that direction.

Realistically, when we listen to the ranting of a Joy Killer, we may actually be hearing a subconscious confession of their inner sorrow and fear to advance in life — a fear that they may want to transfer to others to keep from being left behind as we move forward. Living as though trapped in a cage of endless impossibilities, we can understand why the theme of their discourse is based on discouraging others from taking up any challenge that they have long given up on themselves.

What this means is that the Joy Killer suffers from a kind of mental illness or psychological impediment that we must not mistake as being worldly wisdom. Instead, we should see these acts of mental terrorism as a declaration of their failure to see the value in taking risks as they wait patiently instead for death to relieve them of their misery.

For this reason, it is not wise to engage with such a person for they cannot be convinced that life is a magical gift worthy of our constant unwrapping. Instead, their stubborn resistance to hopeful thinking can leave us feeling angry, frustrated and drained of our last glimmer of hope and enthusiasm for life. As such, if happiness matters to us, then we must learn to avoid this habitual slayer of other people's joy.

Mister Helpless

Profile Overview:

Mister Helpless is another familiar type of energy vampire who we can recognize as any mature adult who pretends to be incompetent or who purposely remains ignorant so that others are forced to make an effort on their behalf. As such, they do not represent a genuine threat but are more an annoying presence in any home or workplace wherein they try to avoid depleting their own energy by taking a passive spectator role, especially when confronted by new challenges or inconvenient tasks.

Familiar Examples:

Mister Helpless will exploit any opportunity to avoid making an effort. This includes using the division of social duties based on gender as the basis to avoid doing particular kinds of work. Subsequently, a man may justify his refusal to clean dishes or do laundry by referring to this as "women's work," whereas a woman may use her femininity as an excuse to not assert her power in society; shrugging it off as a man's duty. And in any strictly patriarchal culture, this is exactly how men want it.

As a way to avoid future exertion, Mister Helpless may also employ various preemptive strategies. This includes avoiding doing something once so that others cannot expect them to do it again — from taking out the garbage to making home repairs. Some men will even leave a sink full of dirty dishes for their wives to clean after she returns home from work — just in case she should begin to expect more of him.

We also find the Mister Helpless energy vampire among those who buy new computers or electronic devices and then expect someone else to read the manual and show them how to use it. In this way, they are able to avoid the mental effort and frustration of having to learn. They may even claim to be "…no good at this kind of thing," which is a true statement for anyone when we avoid improving our skills by never investing the time and effort necessary to get better.

Energy Losses Incurred:
We can already anticipate what kinds of energy losses we might incur in any relationship with the Mister Helpless type. In the most obvious case, we find one marriage partner expending far more time, money and energy to maintain that relationship than the one trying to avoid expending any energy at all. This imbalance in the sharing of duties may eventually have that overworked partner wondering what benefit they derive in maintaining such a one-sided relationship.

This makes it all the more ironic when married couples conspire to create a kind of mother to child co-dependent relationship wherein the wife acts as the mother-figure while her husband assumes the role of a helpless child. In this way, each one is emotionally served in that the woman gains a greater sense of power as the man surrenders his own. However seductive such role-playing games might be, they can also leave one partner disempowered, as when a husband cannot even cook a simple meal for himself, while his wife feels chronically tired and depleted of energy in taking on far too much responsibility.

Outside the home, many citizens choose to play the Mister Helpless role politically by refusing to be socially proactive. Instead, they slouch into the role of being passive followers and ultimately resentful victims of those who are more ambitious and determined to succeed. Their acts betray a motto suggesting that *the best course of action is to take no action at all*. Subsequently, they may even make a great effort to avoid making an effort, a paradox demonstrated by people who will fight to the death in clinging to some convenient and near-thoughtless form of thinking, such as offered by many governments and religious control systems to encourage us not to think for ourselves and just follow orders.

As we can see, it would be easy for any one of us to slip into the role of being a Mister Helpless. And, in certain instances, this will even be encouraged by the more exploitive kinds of energy vampires who want us to believe that we are not "smart enough" to know better and must therefore leave all the most important social and political decisions to them, whether it serves the best interests of all, or only their own.

Energy Vampire Profile

The Poor Rich Man

Profile Overview:
Those who belong to this energy vampire type are legendary for being compulsively stingy despite having great wealth. To better understand such behavior, let us first consider the symbolic meaning of money to those who hoard it far in excess of their actual needs.

To any poor person, money represents basic survival — food, shelter and clothing to keep warm. But to a wealthy person it can represent anything from social dominance and unrestricted power, to attaining freedom from the oppressive constraints of working class life. To a man, it means easy access to the most beautiful women, no matter his age or physical rank. More importantly, it means controlling the destiny of a nation as the owner of its workforce and political decision-makers. In fact, money gives us unfettered access to anything but a meaningful life or an honest friend who we can trust to speak the truth. As for the rest — it can all be easily bought on the open market.

Generosity and sharing, as a human impulse, exists in opposition to the attaining of wealth. And given that the more money we amass, the more power we possess, we can understand why both generosity and sharing are low priorities on the list of many a wealthy person.

To them, money is a strategic weapon used to control their own lives by controlling others. What wealth cannot control, however, is human character — namely the temperament and inclinations with which we are born. As such, we will find wealthy people who are exceptionally kind and generous, while others remain domineering and adversarial in all their private and social relationships.

Among the most significant inclinations we are born with is our fear of dying, which some people feel in excessive of any threat they might be facing. Subsequently, regardless of how great one's fortune may be, they may still feel overly weak and vulnerable. And given that a loss of economic power poses countless threats to our modern-day existence, we can understand how the fear of losing money can manifest even in the mind of the wealthiest person in the form of a "poverty mentality" wherein they can afford every kind of luxury, yet cannot spend their money because this feels like a violent assault upon their well-being.

Notwithstanding greed, which results from a different primal urge, the Poor Rich Man is afflicted with a fear of spending money. And so they live a truly ironic and tragic existence in having great wealth while remaining in a state of spiritual poverty. And from within this state of mind, they take as much as they can from others while giving back as little as possible in return, or preferably — nothing at all.

Familiar Examples:
Henrietta Howland "Hetty" Green has the distinction of being named "the most miserly woman in the world" by the Guinness Book of World Records. She is a well-documented example of the Poor Rich Man energy vampire type. As the wealthiest woman in the United States of the 1800's, she famously took her son to a free clinic for poor people to get his broken leg treated. It was then later amputated because of complications likely due to poor care. She also fought for years to inherit her aunt's estate after learning that it was destined for charity. Making her desperate grabbing all the more tragic is that she was a multimillionaire at a time when the working wage was $1.25/day. In short, she had no logical reason for being so protective of her money.

Poor Hetty's poverty mentality also caused her to wear the same black dress each day until it was too worn out to be repaired. Only then did she spend money on a new one. Obviously she was suffering from some form of mental illness, yet like any wealthy person, society let her to get away with all of it, including tax evasion and forging her aunt's signature to take possession of her $600,000 estate.

Other examples of the Poor Rich Man energy vampire include any wealthy business owner who complains of "hard times" to avoid paying employees a fair compensation for enriching their employer. In fact, if we inventoried their financial holdings we might find enough money to finance a lifetime of high comfort for all their employees and many others besides. Instead, it all goes to one person — and the politicians who facilitate their pathological selfishness by enacting tainted laws.

Energy Losses Incurred:
Driving past urban slums and countryside gated communities, we see how the rich and poor are separated both by geographic distance and also within our minds when we ignore the plight of others across this monumental economic divide. Add to this the rather ironic *desperation for more* that either side can feel and we can understand why social problems of this kind are not as easily solved as the thawing of old Ebenezer Scrooge's heart in Dickens' classic tale, A Christmas Carol.

Herein, a fear for one's own mortality was sufficient to reform the town's most notorious miser. Yet the Poor Rich Man is already fearful of losing their life and economic control. And as in the case of Hetty Green, her pathological stinginess affected not only the quality of life for her society and son, but also for herself in refusing to buy a few more dresses to wear during the week.

In short, there is no easy solution for bringing a wealthy person who fears to share back into the fold of a caring society. Making it worse is that those of lesser means try to ingratiate themselves with the wealthy by offering their services for free, which only further increases their sense of entitlement to more than a fair share of life's bounty.

As such, it is important to acknowledge why societies exist, which is to protect the many and especially the young from adversity. This is a common feature among animal groups in the wild and should be our primary focus as global citizens in every society. Yet in every part of the world we see the wealthy being coddled and celebrated in ways that suggest they are the most valued asset to be protected at the cost of all others, as evident in times of war and recession. It is an attitude that has long destroyed human societies and relationships as those most advantaged fight to retain their power by sacrificing everyone else.

Our only hope in overcoming this problem is to completely reassess how we think as societies; what do we value most: people, or power? And if the latter, then we should all be issued guns so that we can start killing one another to build up our personal wealth. Is that not fair?

The Underwhelming Over-Talker

Profile Overview:

The Underwhelming Over-Talker attempts to keep talking for as long as possible to ensure that we never have a chance to disagree or even speak at all when arguing a point or involved in a debate.

The notion of their being "underwhelming" derives from listening to their arguments. In many cases, the speaker is not a very sophisticated or original thinker, yet their behavior suggests that they believe they have a superior intellect or greater worldly wisdom.

We also get the impression that their unrelenting verbal onslaught is a thinly-disguised attempt to compete for dominance against those who would dare to challenge them to a battle of wits.

Familiar Examples:

The Underwhelming Over-Talker style of behavior will be familiar to us from having watched political election debates wherein candidates make desperate attempts to continue talking long after their allotted time has run out or their point has been made. In reality, they use their incessant banter and onslaught of counter-arguments as a diversionary tactic to deflect information that may contradict their own. In this way, they hope to create the illusion of being the dominant authority figure, whether on the political stage, or at the family dinner table.

Energy Losses Incurred:

Communication is a two way street, yet these energy vampires try to block both lanes to ensure that no one can pass or move ahead. As a result, they are terrible at maintaining relationships that require them to listen and not interrupt others constantly as though to suggest that what the other person has to say is neither important nor worthy of listening to. As such, they will try wear us down so that nothing of genuine merit is ever discussed, whether a lingering marital problem, or changes that need to be made to improve our societies.

CHAPTER 5
The Deniers

CATEGORY DESCRIPTION:
The Denier is someone who willingly rejects any truth or contradiction to their established beliefs to protect their interpretation of reality.

UNDERLYING MOTIVES:
The Denier may want to deny the truth to avoid accepting the blame or consequences of their wrongdoing. They may also want to avoid losing their power or social advantages, or changing a well-worn path of least resistance through life that allows them to make a minimal effort to get what they desire.

METHODS OF MANIPULATION:
The Denier will persist in pretending not to see or understand what we and others clearly do. This allows them to control the outcome of any questioning of their integrity by erecting a barrier of denial between themselves and the truth; a behavior we often see among both career politicians and suspects guilty of a crime.

WEAKNESSES AND VULNERABILITIES:
The Denier fears taking blame or responsibility for any action that may lead to their losing or suffering some undesirable consequence.

NEGATIVE IMPACT ON RELATIONSHIPS:
People who deny the truth or reality itself impede our progress in any kind of relationship. As citizens we cannot solve dire problems related

to pollution if wealthy industrialists deny that such problems exist, or if politicians pretend to be working on our behalf while instead doing the bidding of those who can enrich them. This creates an obstruction of a far greater kind, which is the impeding of our collective conscious and social evolution due to leaders who pretend to be living in denial. This prevents us from improving our world, whether its ailing political systems, broken social infrastructures, corrupted government agencies, or the overwhelmed planetary ecosystems from destructive economic grown policies and careless business practices.

WHO ARE THE DENIERS?

As previously stated, the most common place to find Deniers is among politicians and criminals because both have much to lose. Yet there is no limit as to who can be a Denier given that anyone who wants to maintain a particular status quo will mislead others into believing that there are no reason to change it. As such, it could be a marriage partner denying their infidelity to cling to the economic comforts of a long term relationship or a child lying to its parents to preserve its angelic image within their minds.

Such behavior is problematic given that trust is essential to creating mutually fulfilling relationships. Therefore it is in our collective best interests to be authentic in expressing ourselves to others and making ourselves vulnerable in ways that can prove to be an asset rather than a liability to our relationships. For instance, we should be able to say what we are thinking or feeling as this can only strengthen our bonds with those of equal integrity.

Yet Deniers do not agree with such concepts of submission or retreat from their rigid, fear-based mental stance, no matter how misguided or tragic the consequences to themselves or others. Instead, they will delay the resolution of conflicts by stubbornly clinging to the wreckage of their perceived self-image and the remote promise of its salvation, no matter how rapidly their reputation is sinking before our eyes.

The Always Offended

Profile Overview:
The Always Offended are people obsessed with presenting themselves in a positive light by acting offended by whatever is deemed a negative trait by their peer groups. This includes feigning anger or disgust with opinions, behaviors or any form of expression that opposes the values, beliefs and attitudes of those peer groups, be they political, religious or social organizations of any kind.

At the onset, we need to make a distinction between their behavior and the genuine revulsion we may feel if confronted by something that truly offends us, be it the smell of death, or witnessing violence against a child or animal. Instead, their revulsion is a product of street theatre, wherein the person is making an exaggerated effort to demonstrate their loyalty to their peer group by loudly and publicly displaying their adherence to the values, beliefs and attitudes to which that peer group subscribes. In other words, the issue at hand may be of less importance to them than proving that they belong to that particular group.

At a deeper level, this may be a manifestation of social status seeking wherein individuals and groups compete for rank in the dominance hierarchy of greater society by making their presence known to rivals or peers in the ongoing human competition for power and glory.

Familiar Examples:
In the jargon of social psychologists, there are "in" and "out" groups by which we define our sense of identity in relation to each kind. Simply put, whichever group we belong to is the "in" group and those we reject as not defining our sense of identity are the "out" groups. This simple web of interrelations helps us to understand much of what is going on in regard to our social posturing for dominance or group acceptance.

For instance, it has long been the policy among aristocrats and the culturally sophisticated to shun the poor with whose social values or circumstances they cannot identify. And in an effort to prove their own distance from such people, they must make a show of their revulsion for such people — or conversely, their pity for them by holding costly black tie charity events to which the poor are not invited. Here again, we see that this is more about group posturing than genuine kindness.

In a similar vein, we find religious groups condemning the entire world for not belonging to their "in" group and following its collection of social laws and superstitious beliefs. Here as well, we see expressions of status seeking by those group members who revel in a form of social snobbery that they otherwise could not afford in the real world.

In a further example, positive changes are occurring in our societies due to social media and the internet with regard to the increased reporting of abuses by police, politicians and anyone who could more easily hide their indiscretions from public view in the past. However, some people also exploit the reporting of such crimes or even invent them to draw attention to themselves or their social causes. The result is a reflexive reaction to *always be offended* by those outside our own "in" groups, which leads to the over-reporting and over-accusing of others for the sake of what is often just a self-serving form of street theatre.

Today, we are becoming used to people hating us for being on the wrong side of their mental fence. We may have people belonging to a religious group pointing fingers at us for being "evil" while political extremists may brand us a "baby killer" or "Nazi," depending on how long it takes them to assume our political voting preferences.

Energy Losses Incurred:
The obvious fallout from all of this fake posturing is that anything can potentially be deemed offensive by anyone, which allows the truly offensive aspects of human behavior to lose their power to offend as a result of our being distracted by too many non-issues.

Furthermore, there is a growing "cancel culture" that is doing the equivalent of throwing the baby out with the bath water. The behavior of this over-reaction to being offended is not unlike taking one's car to the scrapyard because the tire is flat. In short, even our response to being offended is highly exaggerated and wasteful to our cultures.

In addition, the Always Offended may show little regard for what are truly significant social offenses perpetrated by their own leaders due to always looking outside the group for any infractions. As an example, a financially-ambitious person may act offended in seeing a poor person sleeping on their street, yet not by the selfish cultural values that cause the vulnerable of society to lose their most basic human comforts.

We also find people pretending to be offended by language in ways that suggest they are actually using those words as an excuse to avoid listening to those speaking to them. In short, they are more concerned with *how* a message is conveyed than its actual content.

This can create unnecessary distractions to our own communications if we overreact to the use of any word on our list of offensive language. We may then sabotage any genuine intimate conversations with others if they are too distracted with censoring themselves just to meet our approval. Nor can we know what the censored are actually thinking.

However, perhaps the greatest loss from people feigning offense to everything around them is that we cannot address critical social issues when we treat everything as a critical social issue — or when others try to keep us from addressing them if they deem such discussions to be too offensive. In this way, the Always Offended energy vampire steals our collective momentum and power to initiate action by stalling us in mid-sentence or mid-progress by pretending to be offended.

To conclude this profile, I offer a parable to demonstrate the irony inherent to the blocking behavior of the Always Offended:

■ ■ ■

A frantic man comes running into the cathedral yelling "Fire! Fire!" whereupon a group of angry priests surround him saying: "How dare you come running into God's house screaming like a wild-eyed savage. You must say three prayers of penance before we will allow you to speak." It was during his second prayer that the burning roof collapsed upon them, despite God having sent a messenger to warn of the impending danger.

■ ■ ■

Energy Vampire Profile

The Ill Informer

Profile Overview:

The Ill Informer is someone who has become addicted to conspiracy theory culture in such a way as to compromise their ability to interact peacefully or unconditionally with others in the world around them.

The irony of their circumstance is that they believe everyone else is ill-informed and therefore naïve. What we may also detect from how they speak to us is an attitude seen among religious snobs and the "Always Offended" types. Here, they will use their "in" group beliefs to mentally elevate themselves above others, thereby revealing conspiracy theory thinking to also be a kind of status-seeking activity. Evidence of this is found in their referring to non-believers as "sheeple," which suggests that those disagreeing with their own conspiratorial beliefs are part of a lowly, obedient herd of ignorant human livestock.

Familiar Examples:

Yes, conspiracies do exist. A sports team is a group conspiracy to defeat other sports teams. Governments are a conspiracy by the powerful to control the land and lives of the less powerful. There are even biological conspiracies, as with the parasite causing Toxoplasmosis, which forces the mouse host to walk into a cat's path to perpetuate its life cycle.

However, we must limit our own wild speculation as to what untold evils lie in waiting for us, especially if our only witness lives inside our imagination or that of others sharing our mental obsession. In fact, the fears we promote may be symptoms of an untreated mental illness.

Energy Losses Incurred:

Like any person who is mentally obsessed, we are often unable to have a flexible, multi-facetted relationship with an Ill Informer because they always lead every conversation back to their favorite obsession. This wastes valuable life energy in both the life of listener and story teller by diverting their attention away from provable social conspiracies.

Energy Vampire Profile

The Illegal Dumper

Profile Overview:

Disagreements are best resolved when both sides remain focussed on the topic at hand. Yet the Illegal Dumper is determined never to take the blame for any wrongdoing and will sabotage the resolution process by "dumping" unrelated grievances into the discourse to distract us.

These manipulative counter-strikes can take the form of accusations about our past behavior or random attacks on our character meant to invalidate our grievances. The true purpose of such attacks is to distract us from the issue at hand by putting us on the defensive or causing our thoughts to veer off to other topics as a result of our emotional reaction to their hurtful criticism. In this way, they can avoid addressing the core issue or dealing with the consequences of being at fault, such as having to change some overtly selfish aspect of their behavior.

The Illegal Dumper is considered an energy vampire for attempting to weaken our self-confidence and inner resolve. In this way, we will not have the emotional strength to prevail in an argument or negotiate from a position of strength in that relationship. Instead, they want to make us overreact so that our behavior becomes the new focus of that argument rather than their own selfish transgressions against us.

Familiar Examples:

Although we may not have given it a name, many of us have been the victim of "illegal dumping" by others in the past. A common example is when someone taunts us with insulting names to weaken our resolve. For instance, many a boy has been called a "wimp" or worse by the local schoolyard bully as he tries to manipulate others into doing what is otherwise against their best interests. In this way, the intended victim is distracted from wanting to avoid risky behavior by a nagging urge to disprove this unflattering claim. And so, in an effort to prove he is not "a wimp," that boy may risk injury or even death by accepting that bully's reckless challenge.

In this example, the bullying Illegal Dumper also avoids having to address the logical argument — "Why should I endanger myself?" by redirecting that child's focus toward the shameful consequences of his refusal to take the challenge — namely, to be labelled a "wimp" in front of his peers. And if girls are present, the pressure to prove himself will increase from his *Bio-Psychological urge to compete for dominance.

Sadly, the maturity level of our discourse as adults may change very little once anger pushes through the veneer of our civility to reveal the raw selfish impulses that are raging just below the surface.

We see this during political debates wherein candidates hoping to avoid a difficult question will instead attack their opponent to create a diversion from having to answer for their personal flaws or failures. As a result, democratic elections become a farce as the focus of the voting public is diverted from critical social issues to those unsavory acts that each candidate accuses the other of having engaged in — and how these alleged weaknesses of character prove them unsuitable for the role of leader in a governing position.

In everyday family life, illegal dumping may occur if a wife asks her husband to begin a promised home repair only to find herself having to defend her failure to honor her own promises of the past. Here, the husband may divert blame away from himself by littering the field with emotional debris from his wife's own past transgressions against him — whether his opportunistic claims are legitimate or not.

Family life is notorious for such subversive attacks as our emotional debts accrue without repayment and family members seize upon every opportunity to air those old grievances to gain a psychological edge during an argument. This not only sidetracks the issue but may also cause either person to walk away to avoid further conflict, thus leaving both sides frustrated and the issue unresolved. And if that issue is met by the same kind of deflecting behavior each time it is raised, then we need not wonder why emotional wounds that have never been given a chance to properly heal may one day begin to fester and turn septic.

Energy Losses Incurred:
Our losses from "illegal dumping" behavior within relationships can be significant. For one, it can leave problems unresolved for years or even decades as we waste our time confronting someone who refuses to face the truth of a dire situation or responds with ridicule to serious issues, not unlike a sadistic bully strutting around in the schoolyard.

In this regard, we also need not wonder why little positive progress is made by governments given the diversionary arguments of political representatives to focus our attention on party loyalty, patriotism or hot topics such as abortion and sexual morality. In this way, they can avoid having to make genuine progress or losing an election for taking a stand that may prove unpopular with their voting base.

Our best option in dealing with an Illegal Dumper is to impose dire consequences for their failing to address any serious problem. In short, if they want to play dirty, they will forfeit the game and lose.

However, this is also why nuclear weapons were invented so that those desperate to win can use our fear of dying against us to ensure their own victory. As a result, our entire nation can be left in a futile holding pattern under the sway of corrupt leaders because we lack the basic political power to do anything about it.

As such, we can take two approaches to these challenges. The first is to not become so dependent upon others that we must surrender our basic freedoms. The second is to implement **Direct Democracies so that we as global citizens can remove the obstacle of selfish people who enter politics only to serve their own best interests. In short, we must start voting for useful ideas rather than useless politicians.

---

*Bio-Psychology is one of the primary topics discussed in my book, Clearing a Path to Joy. It relates to the kinds of behaviors that are subconsciously guided by our instinctual urges to survive and procreate. For example, it causes the urge in adolescent boys to compete for dominance in sports and other activities.

***Citizen Based Social Planning* is a form of direct democracy that you can learn more about at www.rolandk.ca/cbsp

The Minimizer

Profile Overview:

Losing always inflicts some penalty or punishment, and in context of arguments, the loss suffered is a lowering of our stature in the eyes of others. As such, few of us respond well to losing, and the Minimizer least of all. As a highly competitive or controlling person, they simply cannot afford to appear defective or inferior. Subsequently, if forced to take the blame, the Minimizer will attempt to "minimize" their failure by making our grievances seem trivial. And so, after losing a lengthy argument, we might hear them say: "Well, it doesn't matter anyway."

Understandably, being wrong is an unpleasant experience because it implies that something is "wrong" with us. And if others then judge us as being ignorant, incompetent or downright "evil" in our intentions, we will be seen as a liability to society. Therefore, to avoid being caste out as undesirable, we try to minimize our mistakes or transgressions against others to protect ourselves. And in doing so, we may also fail to pay a fair price for the harm we have caused to others.

Familiar Examples:

In the book's introduction, we characterized energy vampires as being people whose instinctual selfishness is so pathological that it eclipses their concern for the well-being of others. As such, while society can teach us to mimic civility by saying "please" and "thank you," there is no denying that some of us are unfit to be trusted in a peaceful society. And so, to avoid this unflattering verdict, the offending Minimizer must invent some plausible excuse to salvage their public reputation.

Among public figures, we hear familiar phrases such as "It was an honest mistake" or "I misspoke" when they are caught in the act. In the case of more violent crimes by tyrannical dictators and wife-beaters, we encounter the DARVO defense wherein the attacker **D**enies their guilt by **A**ttacking the victim's prior behavior, thus **R**eversing the role of the **V**ictim and **O**ffender. In short, whatever crimes they commit are the fault of their victims, including the dead. And so, to save himself the public embarrassment in being labelled a psychotic mass murderer, a tyrant such as Adolf Hitler simply blamed his victims for their being non-Aryan — or disloyal for not wanting to join his death squads.

Yet beneath their acts of mental trickery resides a truth we are not likely to hear confessed: "I am a terrible human being for what I have done and cannot be trusted to protect others in society from my own selfish impulses." Instead, these perpetrators will only further betray our trust with even more lies to conceal this ugly truth.

Energy Losses Incurred:
When a child is born exhibiting pathologically selfish behavior, it can ruin its future chances of establishing intimate, caring relationships because anyone could be their next victim. For instance, they may steal our money or never return items they borrow, thus undermining the bonds of trust so that we never feel entirely safe in their presence. They may then further minimize our avoidance behavior by referring to us as anti-social or "a whiner" who should just "get over it."

In addition, we can lose time, energy and patience trying to secure an admission of guilt from those who never allow themselves to be seen for who they truly are. In some cases, we may waste our entire lives trying to make an honorable person of those without honor, or in hoping for signs of remorse from those who feel nothing of the sort.

In reality, the life of a Minimizer is already a form of punishment for this energy vampire type. After all, we generally will not see them being sincerely joyful or authentic in the presence of others as they are too concerned with their public image. Instead, they are always forced to conceal their true character for fear of being exposed as an impostor. And if exposed, they can become even more repugnant by pretending not to see or understand what everyone else clearly does.

In short, we are best to stay away from such people for they will only continue to betray our trust. And if they are angry for being ignored, they may further blame us, thereby continuing to minimize their own role in creating a life defined by misery and counterfeit smiles.

Energy Vampire Profile

The Selfish Sleeper

Profile Overview:

The Selfish Sleeper is a person whose life has become so structured and predictable in attending to their basic comforts that it gives them little to think about in terms of making choices or even thinking itself.

For the inquisitive, this behavior is documented in *Clearing a Path to Joy* as "comfort-seeking" through the adopting of pre-scripted social identities that use an "IPSFA Sequence" to map out every detail of a person's thoughts and behaviors. For our purposes here, we only need to know that when our thinking becomes rigid, we can no longer adapt in real time to real world circumstances, thus causing conflicts between those who remain spontaneous and mentally flexible and those tied to their unwavering life routines out of existential fear or lifelong habit.

Familiar Examples:

"Fundamentalism" is a familiar example of Selfish Sleeper behavior. Here, the person insists that nothing can change about their religious beliefs or cultural traditions. In this way, every aspect of their lives remains safely predictable so as not to trigger their fear. However, this is also in use as a form of mind control to exploit large groups of people by ensuring that they all think and behave in the same way each day.

Energy Losses Incurred:

The energy lost to Fundamentalism is manifold. The most obvious is to the person whose life is so rigidly programmed, for they leave little room for themselves to learn, grow or discover new things outside of the mental box in which they have warehoused their static lives.

Critical energy is also lost by societies affected by such behavior as social progress cannot be made due to the overly-conservative mindset of people clinging to a scripted life routine designed for comfort rather than a changing world. But the most energy is lost in trying to awaken a Selfish Sleeper who may lash out violently if threatened by change.

Energy Vampire Profile

The Sunshine Messenger

Profile Overview:

The Sunshine Messenger is anyone who exhibits an exaggerated sense of joyful well-being in an effort to mislead us — or themselves — into believing that "everything is perfectly fine" when in fact, it is not.

Aside from television with its overly-cheerful sales presentations, we also find such persons among those trying to deny the reality of living in a troubled world wherein we all can feel overwhelmed at times.

Familiar Examples:

When approached to join a religion, we may encounter people who are suspiciously "too happy" for the occasion. In fact, during recruitment drives, religious cults may send young, attractive Sunshine Messengers to mingle with new prospects to create a false positive first impression of how it feels to be a part of that group; a form of "love-bombing."

Elsewhere, charismatic new age gurus often create an electrified atmosphere of elation among participants at any human potential movement event. Some will seem overly-affected emotionally by all that is happening, which also creates a false positive of that event's true joy potential. At other times, we can encounter people having such an overly-cheerful disposition that it makes them inaccessible to ordinary human conversation about real life problems; as though they are trying to purposely block out every negative aspect of life from their minds.

Energy Losses Incurred:

We must be careful not to reflexively condemn anyone for being "too happy," for there are valid causes for heightened states of euphoria, including spiritual awakenings. Yet those whose joy is an orchestrated pretense are the purveyors of a *toxic positivity* that seeks to deny, ignore or minimize their own and other people's problems in an effort to hide from the truth or even reality itself. As such, they wear happiness like a mask to hide from feelings that they may fear to address.

CHAPTER 6
The Deceivers

CATEGORY DESCRIPTION:
The Deceiver is someone who intentionally manipulates others using fakery and lies.

UNDERLYING MOTIVES:
The Deceiver is typically motivated by profit or a desire to win without having to make an effort or prove their qualifications as a legitimate leader or authority figure. Their motto is "Fake it to make it."

METHODS OF MANIPULATION:
The Deceiver seeks to control others by cheating, lying or obscuring vital information that will cause their legitimate rivals to lose or fail.

WEAKNESSES AND VULNERABILITIES:
The Deceiver fears being exposed for his or her deceptions because that will lead to losing their unfair winning advantage over others.

NEGATIVE IMPACT ON RELATIONSHIPS:
The Deceiver obstructs our ability to succeed in life or negotiate a fair agreement in context of any relationship wherein trust is essential.

WHO ARE THE DECEIVERS?
Like most energy vampires, the Deceiver exploits their relationships with others for personal gain. In doing so, they destroy the bonds of

trust so critical to ensuring a joyful balance in relationships wherein both sides are equally supported in achieving their desired goals.

The Deceiver is an opportunistic liar, whether in trying to evade taking responsibility for their transgressions against others or in trying to mislead us for financial or other kinds of personal gain. They can be a stranger or a family member whose dishonesty becomes a threat to the well-being and stability of our household.

Ironically, there is no law of nature dictating that we must always be truthful in satisfying our personal needs or desires. In fact, nature even seems to reward those animals in the wild who excel at taking unfair advantage of another's gullibility, lack of awareness or life experience. This is evident not only in the stealth hunting tactics of apex predators but also in the use of camouflage and mimicry by insects and invasive parasites to overcome our normal defenses.

However, such stealthy, premeditated feeding behaviors are mostly directed towards other species rather than one's own. Nonetheless, it remains up to each one of us to decide whether walking an honest path is the right choice for the long term goals we hope to achieve.

The Deceiver has made that decision by renouncing honesty and fair play in favor of cheating their way through life. As such, they can also expect to live in a constant state of paranoia in having to always look over their shoulder at a world that mirrors back those same suspicions that they cultivate in the minds of their victims. In short, they cannot trust others for fear of their harboring the same predatory instincts.

Ultimately, the Deceiver can expect to live an unhappy life in never being able to proudly speak of their accomplishments, except to others of their kind and in whose company they are also not to be trusted. In short, they doom themselves to living a lonely and dishonorable life surrounded by people whose motives they also cannot trust.

The Celebrity Tapeworm

Profile Overview:
The Celebrity Tapeworm is any person or media enterprise that uses our attraction to famous celebrities to draw attention to themselves. Like those parasitical tapeworms that latch onto our intestines to get a free meal, so do Celebrity Tapeworms latch onto the public's interest in those with genuine talent, skill or social prominence to ensure their own free meal. In short, they ride the coattails of the rich and famous.

Our fascination with celebrity culture is understandable given that such people often set our social standards for excellence in fields that range from dramatic acting and musical performance to controlling our world as heroic leaders and demented villains. And so it is likewise understandable why we would stop to view something on TV or the internet to learn more about such interesting people.

Also playing a role in drawing our attention is our common interests in money, power, sex and social status. As such, we are more likely to pay attention to those already having what most of us yearn for, which is to be rich, famous or loved by all. And whether we watch out of envy or awe, what we also want to know is: how do *we* compare to *them?*

Familiar Examples:
As movie theaters came into existence, they needed to keep their seats filled to make money. This led to the showing of newsreels featuring sexy movie stars to keep us lining up every weekend to see them. This led to the rise of talk shows and celebrity gossip media through which famous celebrities could instruct their viewing audiences when and where to buy their next ticket.

While celebrity gossip shows are parasitic, their relationship with celebrities is symbiotic in serving the interests of both parties. Yet with the advent of the internet, anyone on a social media platform can use sensationalistic headlines such as "SHOCKING VIDEO OF [insert celebrity's name] SURFACES." to earn vast undeserved sums of money by misleading the public into watching them ramble on for the next twenty minutes about what they think of people who actually do have some unique talent or redeeming quality as an entertainer.

Energy Losses Incurred:
Known widely as "clickbait," what the Celebrity Tapeworm offers is the promise of an entertaining experience that often wastes our time while rewarding them financially for having tricked us into watching.

This forces us to face yet another unsettling aspect of media in that its priority is to sell advertising by luring as many people as possible to view their ads. In other words, the scam artist is as much appreciated by advertisers as the person who has spent years honing their craft to create media content of a socially redeeming or educational quality. In short, their value system cheapens our entire human experience.

And so, while tricking viewers into watching bad content may bring massive economic gains to social media companies and scam artists, it also causes an equally massive loss to our society in terms of our quality of life and the values and standards we may wish to uphold.

For example, should we consider the world's worst guitarist equal to the very best if he can fool enough people into buying tickets to their shows? Or should we consider an auto mechanic the equal of a brain surgeon if he can trick others into letting him operate on their brains? And finally, should we allow anyone to become the leader of a nation just because they are rich or famous enough to win more votes than the legitimate candidates? As we have all seen, such things can happen.

And while lowering our standards can make overnight media stars of the ordinary and mediocre, it does not change the fact that it also lessens the value of our human experience by undermining our quest for excellence. As such, we should all be asking ourselves: *What kind of world do I want to live in?* And then act accordingly.

Energy Vampire Profile

The Crooked Crusader

Profile Overview:
The Crooked Crusader is someone who exploits worthy social causes for their own benefit by drawing public attention and financial aid to themselves. In doing so, they often exhibit behavior associated with The Hypocritic energy vampire type by desecrating the very values that they claim to uphold whenever they are not in the public eye.

Familiar Examples:
During our yearly Earth Day celebrations around the world, we will not only encounter genuine advocates for planetary sustainability and the environment but also people who exploit this cause for their own selfish advantage by masquerading as an ambassador for those values. We may then find someone offering beautiful paintings of our world with emotionally-charged messages of support for the cause, yet once home they throw their metal cans and other reusable materials into the regular trash because they have no desire to make any effort on behalf of our planetary ecosystems to recycle those items responsibly.

A more familiar example finds people selling bracelets or other kinds of jewelry on social media sites under the guise of helping to save the oceans or animals. Yet when visiting their websites, we find a catalogue for selling merchandise but little proof of their being involved in some activity to benefit the environment. Tell-tale signs of this scam are its exploiting of the latest unfolding crisis with a website that was recently registered and has no useful contact information. By comparison, any legitimate charity will often have a decades-long internet presence.

Energy Losses Incurred:
The loss is felt by all of humanity as we put our faith in opportunistic grifters who steal our money and destroy our trust in the credibility of legitimate charities working to make our world a healthier place for all of us to live in. Ultimately, we all must breath the same air...

Dr. Death Defier

Profile Overview:

Dr. Death Defier is a con artist who exploits elderly people's fear of dying to sell them fake miracle cures that promise to treat every kind of ailment and even reverse the aging process itself.

Familiar Examples:

Once an elderly person gets on a mailing list for health products, they can expect to also get direct mail advertisements from companies with dubious credentials and a P.O. Box address making claims that their health products are made by leading medical experts and can cure any ailment from memory loss and arthritis to sexual dysfunction. None of this is true, but to an elderly person terrified of dying, these hucksters are the only "experts" willing to promise what they cannot have, which is their former health and youthful vitality returned for the price of a few bottles of useless…(whatever it is that they put in there).

Energy Losses Incurred:

Elderly victims of the Dr. Death Defier energy vampire type may lose vast sums of their pension money buying miracle cures for a condition that has no legitimate known treatment — namely, the slow, deliberate deterioration of our bodily functions due to the aging process.

Unfortunately, people who fall for such lies can be as stubborn as any member of a religious cult in clinging to their faith in these magic potions. This is due to an elaborate system of belief created to keep our faith in such products, including that "they" — the evil medical empire — is the true enemy who will stop at nothing to keep the true healers of this world — like our good Dr. Death Defier — from doing what is in their selfless nature to do — which is to cure old people of dying.

In short, if you receive such advertisements in the mail, report them to the post office as mail fraud, and then throw them in the nearest recycling bin so that something useful can be done with the paper.

The False Profit

Profile Overview:

Religious scripture is quick to warn us of outsiders in the guise of "false prophets" who will lead us astray. This makes it all the more ironic when we find them instead among the leaders of those same religions. As a result, greater humanity has been witness to centuries of parasitic grifting and killing sprees by psychopaths cloaked in the respectable veneer of a major religion through which they were able to rape and pillage the lives of unsuspecting followers.

Adding to this problem is that we cannot easily distinguish between cults and religions, given that both want to keep us under their mental influence. We also find cults borrowing the foundational beliefs of a major religion to create splinter groups of exploitation wherein leaders may suffer from delusional forms of mental illness that have followers committing acts of suicide or murder as an expression of their faith.

Today, many such crimes against our humanity go undetected, lest those cults suffer a psychotic break from reality that wins them a few days of infamy on the evening news. Unfortunately, by the time their crimes are discovered, it is often too late for the victims.

But most tragic of all is that we continue today to wander into the selfish lairs of these shameless fleecers of the human flock to sacrifice our incomes, labor, sexuality or even our lives in an act of blind faith.

Familiar Examples:

Lest we forget, we humans are a status-oriented species, which is why many of us would accept a role in society wherein we are worshipped as someone "special." And if this position pays a high salary, then who could resist? Subsequently, we can find "False Profits" of every kind in our societies who claim to wield special powers or have a direct line of communication with God or angelic space beings. In short, the sky has never been the limit when it comes to duping the masses for profit.

Today, we have leaders in both politics and religion whose followers believe them to have God-like powers over their destiny. Yet the most familiar are the Christian "televangelists" who extort vast sums of money from their elderly victims by convincing them that they will be healed of illnesses or ensured the best seat in Heaven based on the size of their donations. Unfortunately, most will go to their graves without realizing they were the victims of a long-standing confidence scam.

Energy Losses Incurred:
Money and time are the two most obvious losses in being hustled by grifters who sustain our believe in the false realities they create. In the meantime, they travel in private jets wearing the kind of high profile jewelry typical of monarchs and crime bosses. In short, it is a criminal racket that fleeces the weak of body and weak of mind.

But blaming the victims is not entirely fair. After all, the everyday stresses of social life are enough to have us seeking temporary refuge from our suffering in various forms. This is evident in our widespread abuse of alcohol, drugs, pornography and video gaming, all of which provide a kind of alternate fantasy world whose rewards often surpass those offered by the one in which we live. And then there is death, which destroys the life we have spent decades to perfect. Nor has our survival instinct ever accepted our final fate. So why would we give up our lifelong struggle to live without a fight? And there awaits religion, ready to promise us a miraculous healing or an eternal life.

In addition, legitimate remote communities are often created for those who want to escape the hostility and madness of modern society. Unfortunately, some of these communal retreats offer a world of even greater hostility and madness at the hands of self-appointed "masters" presiding over everyone else's lives and right to exist.

In one famous case, such a madman catalogued his mental delusions in book form so that others could perpetuate his psychosis as though it were the spiritual key to the salvation of our world.

Yet ultimately, our way forward in any society is to select leaders of sound mind to administer our collective vision and to demand proof of anyone's Heaven before putting our money down to buy a ticket.

The Fame Facilitator

Profile Overview:
The Fame Facilitator is a con artist who promises us fame and fortune to exploit us for money, sex or other personal gain. As one of many charismatic peddlers of false hope, they typically masquerade as an entertainment or fashion industry insider who claims to have the kind of connections that can get us "to the top." Instead, they will just keep taking our money until we finally realize that we are being conned by an opportunistic social predator.

Anyone can fall victim to this type of energy vampire, but especially those who are young, naïve or in denial about their limited market potential as a fashion model or entertainment superstar. In the real world, such people would encounter a lot of painful rejection. And this is why the Fame Facilitator is so successful because he or she will tell anyone who comes through their front door that they can become as big a star as any of their favorite idols. In this way, their victims can be manipulated into spending vast sums of money to launch a career that will only ever exist within their wishful imagination.

Familiar Examples:
In any major city we find ads calling for "fashion models" that use the promissory hook of "high pay, lots of travel" to lure unsuspecting new victims. Such ads often lead us to a fake modeling agency that makes its money by charging large sums of money to create a "portfolio" for girls who are tricked into believing that they can be a famous fashion model. However, their portfolio will at best be circulated only among family, friends and neighbors rather than any famous fashion designer or movie mogul who is always rumored to be "holding their breath" in anticipation of seeing their finished portfolio.

In this racket, fame is always just one more hefty payment or sexual favor away. And until that young woman or man has the courage to free their mind from the grasp of this self-serving delusion, they may lose both their money and faith in humanity in the lair of this cunning energy vampire. In the meantime, they must keep paying to prolong this enchanting fairy tale with its inevitable unhappy ending.

The music industry offers another venue of exploitation. Here the Fame Facilitator is typically a low level manager or booking agent who signs a multitude of musical acts to generate as much commission for themselves in the short term without regard for the long term careers of their clients. Instead, their strategy is to keep making big promises to keep their ambitious clients trying to bite an invisible carrot. In this way, this grifter keeps performers touring for slave wages while they use their commissions to put a new pool in their backyard or pay off their new sports car. Driven by the desire for more money, they often rig kickback schemes wherein a band pays full price for various rentals or services from which that grifter is paid a further commission.

Energy Losses Incurred:
Not everyone in the entertainment industries is a selfish parasite, but it pays to look out for them if this is where you intend to seek a future. In the examples cited, the energy lost to a Fame Facilitator is primarily our money and the time that we have wasted in being strung along by empty promises. Ultimately, we gain nothing more than heartache and humiliation in return for being financially drained by someone whose only power is in their ability to keep us believing their lies.

A further loss comes courtesy of our being lulled into a self-serving fantasy world that distracts us from using our own initiative to further our career. For instance, a band might have achieved greater success by not wasting time allowing some unscrupulous grifter to drain them of their time, money and enthusiasm. Likewise, a young girl who enters into an agreement with a fake modeling agency will be distracted from entering the real world where she might at least experience an honest rejection by a professional agent rather than a conditional acceptance based on her ability to pay a petty criminal for their useless services.

The Gaslight Girl

Profile Overview:
The term "gaslighting" defines behavior wherein others try to make us disbelieve our direct experiences of what is true or real. The Gaslight Girl does this by concealing her true unsavory nature from a romantic partner, often to cling to that relationship while seeking a new partner who will be unaware of her unflattering character flaws.

While the name suggests a female perpetrator, both genders will use gaslighting within a relationship if it is in their character to do so.

Familiar Examples:
The Gaslight Girl is motivated not by love but self-preservation. As such, even her displays of kindness or caring may be an act to keep her relationship partners passive and under her control.

And if she engages in sexual activity with new recruits for a future relationship, she will conceal her indiscretions by gaslighting a current partner into doubting her infidelity — even as the evidence begins to mount. As such, her success depends on a victim who fears to leave that relationship, or lacks the intelligence to see through her lies.

Energy Losses Incurred:
As the unwitting victim of this energy vampire type, an obvious loss is being with someone who is dishonest and insincere. This dooms every such relationship to failure as it is built on a foundation of sociopathic bluffing and risk-taking behavior that sacrifices future stability for short-term gains. In short, such unions resemble a house of cards.

Gaslighting behavior breeds distrust in our relationships and causes us to live in an alternate reality to maintain those illusions upon which our counterfeit relationship depends — "She really is a *good* person."

Additional losses include the years we often waste in being with the wrong person. And in more tragic cases, we find ourselves being in love with someone who we never really knew — a complete stranger.

The Hungry Shopper

Profile Overview:

When we enter a grocery store feeling hungry, it may cause us to buy food items that we otherwise would never have thought to buy and may later never eat. Feeling empty and "in need of energy" can change our behavior in many ways, as we can become more impulsive and less discerning *in choosing what to bring back home with us.*

The Hungry Shopper energy vampire is a person who is habitually careless in choosing relationship partners, often out of their desperate feelings of loneliness or a fear of not having their existence validated by another's acceptance. This results in opportunistic, impulse-driven sexual encounters leading to short-term parasitic relationships that drain the life and happiness out of both partners.

Familiar Examples:

A hunger for energy in any form can cause us to exhibit behaviors that may not be flattering to our self-worth or spiritual well-being. We can be driven both by physical and emotionally hungers, including feelings of loneliness, sexual arousal, or fearful pressures felt from a demanding parent or culture. This may then cause us to hastily choose a partner for an intimate relationship who we never would have considered had it not been for a nagging feeling of desperation urging us on.

Energy Losses Incurred:

The losses incurred by such behavior mirror those of buying food that we have no intention of eating. Here, both partners sacrifice their joy and future relationship successes by clinging to a sinking ship that will suck their lives into a hopeless abyss of growing frustration and daily resentment. In short, none of us should ever choose in haste whenever that choice truly matters, especially to our long-term happiness. And if we continue to choose otherwise, then we should stop looking to others for a while and spend some more quality time with ourselves.

Mister Quick And Easy

Profile Overview:

In my book *Clearing a Path to Joy,* our complex human relationship to energy is analyzed in vivid detail, and also our attributed susceptibility to greed, vanity and other unsavory mental states. Yet for our purposes here, we need only note that survival is our primary goal in life, which has become inextricably linked to making money in a modern world; a symbolic form of energy used in trading for genuine energy forms.

As an energy-consuming biological system, it is also important that we conserve energy by making the least effort to accomplish any task. This is why we instinctively seek a life of *convenience.* This also causes us to be more selfish and develop familiar habits and routines to make life less energy-draining. In recognizing that these internal impulses rule our lives, we can then understand the logic of how *Mister Quick and Easy* and others of his kind have come into existence.

Mister Quick and Easy is someone who promises to fulfill our need to survive with greater ease and comfort while making that lifestyle quick and easy to achieve. In this way, we need not waste our precious time or energy having to work for it. Naturally, his offer sounds very appealing as a strategy for life — were it not all a blatant lie.

At best, Mister Quick and Easy is greatly exaggerating our chances of realizing a favorable outcome by wasting our time and money on his "success strategy" products and services. His sales pitch exploits the same hope tactics that have us wasting our money on lottery tickets or trying to win oversized stuffed animals at a local fair. Everything is a sure thing until we pay for it. Instead, we learn a costly lesson in that all such incredible money-making opportunities are meant to make only one person rich in a quick and easy manner, and that is Mister Quick and Easy himself. And the quicker we learn this lesson, the more money we can keep out of his frantically grasping hands.

Familiar Examples:
We can find the Mister Quick and Easy energy vampire type at every level of society. He is atop any pyramid investment scam that exploits our economic ambitions and turns us into recruiters to find even more unwitting victims to lose their money. And once his bubble of illusion begins to burst, he is quick to disappear, taking with him our hopes for quick riches and leaving us with only debts and regrets.

His ruse is always the same in searching for new prey among those eager to increase their social status or income to unrealistic levels they might otherwise never achieve. The labor class is an obvious target in having access to credit but never enough money to live a comfortable and carefree life. As such, we can recognize this energy vampire type by their offering "too good to be true" returns for what we are asked to invest in terms of time and money — as evident in ads that promise to pay us $5000/wk to work part-time from home. His hook is always an excessively high return to draw us in because we all want more money without the inconvenience of changing our lifestyle to earn it.

Not everyone falls for his scams, but more than enough of us do to keep Mr. Quick and Easy buying media ads and renting out local halls. He then shows up wearing the kind of expensive clothes and jewelry that draw us further into his illusion of being a "self-made man."

We find Mister Quick and Easy among other energy vampire types including "Dr. Death Defier," who sells quick and easy miracle cures to the elderly using their desperation for relief from suffering and that no legitimate medical treatment can achieve the results promised by this con artist and his modern-day version of snake oil quackery.

Another familiar example is the religious charlatan who promises us quicker and easier access to Heaven in return for sending our money to him. Ironically, we often find these fake spiritualists living the kind of vanity-drenched life of privilege of which at least one religion warns that they have less chance of entering into heaven than a camel has of squeezing through the eye of a needle. But then again, such people are unlikely to believe what is written in those religious books they carry.

Energy Losses Incurred:
Looking at this issue from a limited "legal" perspective, we might be fooled into seeing the losses incurred as transactional and only by the victims of the crime. We can get a more comprehensive viewpoint if we imagine ourselves as a young person growing up in a world built on a foundation of warfare and slavery. Here, where government is but a thinly veiled form of racketeering that can take as much as 90% of our taxable income at will, we are also taught about morality by religious clergy who want to oppress the female gender or may even be exposed as sexual predators of children. Here, where wealthy bankers decide our future by who stays rich or poor, we are also treated like herds of economic cattle by marketers hawking products we don't need by making us afraid of being without them, as with beauty products, etc.

And then, along comes a smooth-talking, charismatic individual promising an escape from this working class nightmare — a means to buy back our freedom from the employers who own us. How could we not be tempted by the opportunity to have someone help us gain our financial independence? But rather than help us, they help themselves to our money, leaving us not only poorer, but with less faith in a world whose biggest winners are the ones running the biggest public scams.

Trust — this is what we are losing, each and every day. And the true costs of this are on a massive scale and unrecoverable.

Meanwhile, to make their crimes more palatable to themselves, the Mister Quick and Easy types of this world tell themselves "If I don't take their money, somebody else will" — a twisted logic akin to saying: "If I don't rape my sister, somebody else will" Yet this is how people try to trick themselves into believing that the crimes they commit against their own humanity are justified so that they can wake up each day to such the last droplets of hope and happiness from our ailing world.

Yes, thinking our way through this labyrinth of corruption can feel like *heavy lifting* to our brains. But it would do all of us a world of good to give some thought as to whether we are lessening the suffering of others, or only making things worse. After all, it's your world too. In what ways do you wish things could be better for all of us?

The Nonsense Seer

Profile Overview:
Superstition and mysticism have been aspects of everyday human life since the days of the tribal witch doctor who interacted with the spirit world on everyone's behalf. This provides a perfect cover and lucrative opportunity for the Nonsense Seer who pretends to have supernatural powers of this kind in order to take advantage of the superstitious and those grieving the loss of a loved one. We typically find such a person acting as a psychic forecaster of romantic futures, a translator for the dead, or an overpriced remover of "curses" placed upon us by others.

Familiar Examples:
Disbelief is the world's most unreliable scientific instrument. Today, as even governments release evidence of UFOs and reputable hospitals conduct clinical research into the afterlife, there is good reason for us to remain open-minded and humble where such beliefs are concerned.

That said, con artists likely outnumber legitimate experiencers of the supernatural by the same ratio as faked UFO videos outnumber the genuine article. Subsequently, we may encounter far more people who claim to have supernatural powers yet whose only true gift is to relieve others of their money without offering anything of value in return.

We can also blame the Nonsense Seer for our collective prejudice against any legitimate claims of supernatural abilities, not only because their fraudulent enterprise is so prevalent, but also because they are so shameless in preying upon the vulnerable in their time of need.

Energy Losses Incurred:
Money is the obvious loss in being duped by fake mystics. Yet they do equal damage to the legitimate study of psychic abilities just as faked UFO videos taint the serious study of a phenomenon that may turn out to be humankind's most significant scientific discovery. In the meantime, when in doubt, listen to your intuition — and only yours.

Energy Vampire Profile

The Sexual Decoy

Profile Overview:
The Sexual Decoy is any young, attractive woman used to trick people into being the audience for a sales or media presentation. An attractive man may also be used, but the female variety is far more prevalent.

The term *decoy* comes from those fake replica animals used by sport hunters to lure the real ones close enough to become their prey. The same strategy is employed by marketers and retailers to ambush their human prey into consuming various goods and services. But what they hunger for is not our flesh and blood, but its symbolic equivalent in the form of our money — or perhaps to influence our thinking.

It is no mystery why heterosexual men respond to young attractive females with sexual interest — their biology promotes such behavior. So rather than restate the obvious, let us focus instead on the far more critical relationship between ordinary women to these vibrant young models with their artificially-enhanced facades of perfection.

What we discover is that female Sexual Decoys are being used to drain women of energy by diminishing their self-esteem. In short, they act as energy vampires for their employers. Their role is to make other women feel inferior in competing for social attention. Once suitably deflated and fearing imminent loss, she can then be induced to buy cosmetics or fashion products that promise to put them back in the race for a storybook happy ending of love, marriage and romantic bliss in the arms of a handsome prince. And all she must do to get what she wants is to spend her weekly pay at the makeup counter.

We can understand the historic importance of women being able to arouse men's sexual attention when we consider that they had long been kept from entering the male-dominated workforce to earn their own living and economic freedom. This is still true in many cultures where men essentially control all aspect of a woman's life. And so the importance of being able to attract a male breadwinner remains a high priority for many women. And where there is competition, there are opportunists promising us victory for a price. But in this case, they sell women products to help them look more like those Sexual Decoys to which they were methodically exposed since childhood by the makers of those products. In other words, they have rigged the system from the start for themselves to become the ultimate winner.

Again, for those interested, my book *Clearing a Path to Joy* exposes these underhanded marketing tactics used in gender politics and the selling of needless products and services to consumers.

Familiar Examples:
Considering the massive profits to our manipulators and the potential damage to the human psyche, we can think of the Sexual Decoy as a covert asset in a psychological war against the public. Using military grade marketing tactics, they urge our minds into compliance with the will of those having economic or even socio-political interests in our buying various products or adopting their social values and attitudes.

We may not speak of the beauty industry in such terms, yet it is every bit as lucrative as the selling of arms to an equally insecure clientele of powerful men fearing defeat at the hands of their own enemies.

As such, the Sexual Decoy is heavily deployed, especially on covers of women's magazines where she is surrounded by subversive calls for women to worry about "What turns him on?" or how to "Pleasure him the right way." All of this visual and mental signaling works in tandem to undermine a woman's confidence both in her appearance and ability to bring value to an intimate relationship. The result is that she will be induced to buy that magazine and its advertised products and perhaps even adopt its values, beliefs and attitudes, much to the detriment of all womankind as she begins to discard her true identity.

Conversely, a magazine featuring plain-looking women and articles that advise her to "just be yourself" are of no use to those chemical and fabric industries hoping to sell their war paint and protective armor to women by making her feel she is under attack by her female rivals and in danger of falling behind in the race for love and happiness.

Energy Losses Incurred:
This mental assault against women penetrates to a far deeper level than we may realize in that it distracts her from seeking true power over her own destiny by making it her highest priority to please men instead. This is also occurring at a time when women are venturing deeper into a once male-dominated workforce to claim ever-higher positions of power in many professions, including law and politics. As such, are her media-based advisers suggesting that she should be more concerned with choosing the right hair or lipstick color, or ensuring her cleavage is sufficiently exposed to improve her skills in managing men?

Yet we must not blame the attractive young models being employed as Sexual Decoys, for they are no more at fault than those inanimate ducks deployed by hunters. They, too, are just a product of our cultures and are also seeking only to win their own fair share of male attention so that they can reap its rewards in the form of a higher income and a glamorous life of travel and constant male attention.

However, we must not ignore their obvious psychological impact upon other women, especially young adolescent girls who may come to hate themselves for not comparing favorably to these artificially over-enhanced misrepresentations of real womanhood. What they and all young girls need are strong, heroic role models, not caricatures of femininity hobbling around on plastic stilts with legs bared for quick, easy access to her most valuable social asset. And never in the media is her intellect given equal attention to that of her hair and nails.

And here we find the source of greatest energy loss for all women in that they are systematically being trained to aspire to a counterfeit embodiment of female empowerment that puts the focus not on her mind, goals or achievements, but on her ability to attract men.

Subsequently, we find women spending inordinate amounts of time obsessing about their appearance. In doing so, they also sideline their intellectual and political development while becoming dependent on external validation to compensate for the loss of self-esteem to a media based campaign of gender degradation since early childhood. In this way, she may come to feel deeply insecure about her worth to society, making her an easy target for industries to prey on her income by way of her low self-esteem.

Moreover, while she is being cleverly distracted, men continue to rule our societies in ways that suggest that the best way forward is to keep repeating the past. In short, we can expect nothing to change.

And finally, in teaching women to become caricatures of femininity, men are likewise taught to aspire to caricatured portrayals of ultimate manhood that are the polar opposite of their female counterparts.

In this way, we are all being driven like herds of human cattle toward a life of spending our time and money chasing happiness in the wrong direction — while those sitting atop the social pyramid must surely be laughing to themselves about all of it — at our expense.

CHAPTER 7
A Word About Victimhood

We have explored the profiles of some of the worst kind of people that we could ever imagine. And while this has given us many insights into the behavior of the perpetrators, our journey would not be complete if we did not also give some thought as to the behavior of the victims of these energy-based crimes.

After all, energy vampires survive by preying upon new victims; they need someone to exploit in order to gain their power, just as a parasite needs a host to feed on for its own continued survival.

This brings us to a rather uncomfortable topic wherein we find that some people are willing victims or at least willing accomplices in their own downfall at the hands of their exploiters. And while our reasons for staying in any abusive or unbalanced relationship can vary based on our unique circumstances or even our culture, we cannot dismiss that there is some degree of accountability for each negative outcome if we chose to do nothing to help ourselves or ignored all the warning signs.

As such, let us now gain additional insight into the energy vampire phenomenon by considering the kinds of circumstances in which we can be more easily exploited. In this way, we might extricate ourselves or someone we care about from a state of victimhood.

While some of these topics have been touched upon in the profiles of various energy vampires, there are some surprises here that might make you think twice about how to react the next time you encounter these situations in your everyday life.

Money Scams

It is worth mentioning again and again that the victims of any kind of "get rich quick" scam always enter into that relationship hoping to earn far more money than they deserve for their meager efforts. In other words, they want an unrealistic return that is out of proportion with their actual level of participation in that scheme. In this way, these transactional relationships begin with unrealistic expectations, thereby paving the way for a future crash landing into bitter disappointment.

It is our entering into this "big dream" state of mind that will keep us giving our money to the perpetrators of these money-based scams. Not long afterward — once we begin to suspect that something is not right but are too timid to speak out — we will enter a second phase. Now, instead of being driven by hope and a lust for material gain, we are driven by fear into a more defensive state of mind. At this stage, we begin counting our losses and start to worry about getting our money back — which rarely happens because the grifters running these kinds of money scams have been through this stage with many others and know how to handle anxious "investors."

What we must be aware of is that when this new emotional dynamic takes over, it can keep us trapped in that energy-draining relationship even longer. As an analogy, let us imagine ourselves as a casino gambler who is starting to lose too much money at black jack. Once we reach this threshold, hope turns to fear and we become less concerned with winning the pot and far more anxious to *break even* by winning our lost money back. This is the secondary psychological trap that awaits us, because we may then spend even more money in trying to break even. This results in losing our initial amount and spending even more to win it all back. And all the while, those who own the casino will continue to take our money day after day, year after year, by exploiting the two common dynamics of human psychology to which we all can easily succumb — hope and fear.

Our reason for getting involved in any kind of a shady deal may even be honorable — perhaps we want to do well for ourselves so that we can give those we love a "better life." But we must also be realistic, for why would a total stranger offer to help us become financially secure for so meager an investment? Realistically, any independently wealthy individual would not ask us for a few thousand dollars. In that world, this is petty cash — lunch money for any vain spender. It therefore makes no sense why a successful person would approach a poor person for money. Instead, they would be looking to those with more money than they have, such as investment bankers, etc.

And yet many of us will continue to hope against all odds and reason for such unlikely miracles to come true. Instead, we will discover that our grifter friend has been making similar promises to others in their attempts to relieve as many people as possible of their money. In many cases, their motive is a simple one in that they are financing a nagging drug or gambling addiction that also has them constantly losing.

In every society we can find musicians, writers or other artistic types who knowingly sacrifice a future life of predictable comfort to follow their dreams. And despite their lifelong commitment and investment in time, many never gain the success they had hoped for, even if they deserve it. Yet their kind of ambition and integrity of vision is a far cry from what we see among the victims of money-based scams. Here, we find instead the kind of people who did settle for a life of comfort but who also want to "make it big" by way of a shortcut that allows them to cling to their comfortable lifestyle. Such a level of commitment is not a true sacrifice but rather an attempt to get *something for nothing;* an attitude that can lead to our downfall if approached by those who sense that we have no genuine ambition and would rather attain a life of luxury in some convenient, effortless way. And what could be easier than to make it *someone else's responsibility* to make us rich?

As the essence of stock trading and human laziness, what awaits us in awakening from this wishful dream state is an ugly truth: getting rich is not easy. Nor would any truly wealthy person waste their time chasing after our meager savings. And while it may flatter our ego, the fact of being named their *exclusive client* may be our worst luck ever.

Hitting the Jackpot

On a related note, any time we play the lottery, our odds of winning the jackpot for this low-level of investment is approximately one in every fifteen million attempts, give or take a few million. On the other hand, the odds that those running the lottery will make millions every week from selling tickets to people just like us are 100% — guaranteed.

For this reason, they also behave like energy vampires by feeding on our hopes, dreams or our desperate desire to escape the hand to mouth existence of being a poor working class slave. This also explains the use of visual appeals in lottery advertising wherein we are enticed to buy tickets by showing us tempting images of beautiful new homes, cars, yachts and exotic vacations while the word "freedom" as used to trigger our want for what every working class slave yearns for; to buy our life back from our economic masters.

Where lotteries are concerned, our losses are strictly voluntary in that no one is forcing us to gamble our weekly income away. On the other hand, our only reason for buying a lottery ticket is to win the big jackpot. For this reason, no lottery company would dare to show us a commercial wherein people are jumping up and down for joy in having won a free ticket or minimum payout of $10.00. Yet that is what the majority (roughly 14,999,999) of us ticket buyers can expect in return for a lifetime of hoping to win big — if we are lucky.

Lottery companies must themselves gamble on the fact that most of us would rather do nothing to get rich than risk changing our life to improve our chances of success. And so, if we counted up our winnings over a lifetime of buying lottery tickets, we may discover that we have spent many thousands of dollars that in retrospect would have been better spent on our child's higher education, on renovating our home to increase its value, or taking a night course on how to get rich in a far more practical way — like inventing something useful to sell.

But until we reach this point in our conscious evolution, we may continue using our money to win free tickets while enriching the true winners of this grift against the poor — the sellers of false hope and those governments that take a piece of the action for making it legal.

Will You Save Me?

Turning our attention now to more personal matters, some of us will find ourselves in relationships where the other person has no genuine concern for our well-being — except insofar as how it interrupts our ability to serve their needs. In the worst of cases, we have married an undiagnosed psychopath who takes pleasure in causing us to suffer as proof of their power over us. Yet what all such tainted unions have in common is that our needs will be ignored in serving those of others. In short, we will live as though we neither exist nor matter.

As a tribal species, we have long depended on the presence of others, not only to help us survive, but also to help us feel less alone. As such, we instinctively seek companionship not only to share the burdens of daily life, but also out of a spiritual need to commune with others. And as we reach out, we may find ourselves in the presence of one of the many types of energy vampires.

While we may sense an exploitive imbalance from the start, the more seductive energy vampire types will lull us into a false sense of security before they strike. Going against their own selfish inclinations, they will pretend to support us in our hopes, dreams and future aspirations. This will trick us into feeling an emotional connection for someone who may actually feel nothing at all.

However, our focus here is not on their behavior, but ours in context of such abuse. Here we begin to find clues as to why things can turn out far worse for victims than they ever should, had we acted earlier or taken a more reasonable approach. Yet like a gambler chasing after lost money at the gaming tables, so do we have the same tendency to cling to relationships in hoping to recover what we have lost or what was never meant to be, such as the love of someone psychologically unable to feel such life-enhancing emotions. And if they are mentally ill or otherwise incapable of better behavior, then it is also not their fault for succumbing to impulses that may turn out to be our undoing. As such, we must be vigilant to not sacrifice our future happiness or well-being for a lost cause — just because we cannot summon the courage to walk away from our own relationship gambling table.

This is also where things can get complicated. After all, the women of many cultures and religious sects are still raised from childhood to see themselves as slave-like servants to men. This goes even further in situations wherein parents select their daughter's future husband or a marriage takes place *before* the couple has even met to test each other's suitability as a life partner. As such, if a woman finds herself trapped in a union wherein she is being abused by her husband, she may see as an obstacle not only her own lack of money or options for escape, but also the selfish demands of her parents or entire culture to keep her in a position of victimhood. After all, a man's future is all that matters.

And so, what often happens is that she will live a life of cowering in misery to avoid the worst of these outcomes, including death. Instead, she must only think of her own safety or that of her children. While those other selfish parties will survive their disappointment, what she cannot survive is her own death at the hands of a man who may see her only as human livestock or a disobedient slave.

But even worse than having our self-esteem diminished at a cultural level — as remains the plight of many women even today — is when we feel no value in our own existence. We may then settle for the worst of everything, from a terrible marriage partner to a low quality of life at home under the false assumption that we are not worth making the effort to escape our miserable circumstances. This makes it easy for any self-serving energy vampire to abuse us and for us to justify their abuse in believing that we are not worthy of better treatment.

And so, whether we are motivated by guilt, shame, pride or any other feeling, what we often find is that the people who suffer most are often as much a part of their undoing as those mistreating them. That is not always the case, but when it appears that there is a greater advantage in staying with our abuser — such as avoiding uncertainty, the ire of our angry parents or even feeling like a "loser" for being single — then we might make the kind of decision that could ultimately leave us with no more decisions to make.

But we must never allow that to happen. Instead, by taking decisive action now, we can make sure that it never will.

Index

aging 33, 56
betrayal v, 18, 27, 47
censorship. See: offend, government
charlatan. See: religion
communication 36, 41, 57
con artists 66
crime 4, 40, 46, 57
dating. See: relationships
domination 10, 12, 18, 21, 36, 39, 67, 69
Dracula myth 9–10
environmental causes 55
fear 4, 15–16, 19–20, 25, 33, 37–38, 42, 45, 47–48, 51, 56
gambling 73–74
government 2, 5, 42, 45, 66
greed 12, 34
investments 13, 64, 73–74
lying 4, 51, 56, 60, 63
marriage 13, 38, 76
medical 56
money 1, 10, 12, 15, 33–34, 47, 53–54, 56, 58–60, 63, 66–67, 70, 72, 76
new age 22, 49
offend 16, 29, 39–42, 46
politics 2, 13, 36, 38–39, 44–45, 58, 68
prejudice 2, 6, 22, 66
psychics 66
relationships vi, 13, 15, 19–20, 25, 32–33, 35, 37–38, 42–43, 45, 47, 51–53, 61, 68, 71–72, 75
religion 11, 22, 57–58, 76
scams 4, 54, 72
self-esteem 1, 18, 23, 67, 69–70, 76
selfishness 1–3, 7, 15, 21, 28, 35, 43–44, 46–48, 76
trust 1, 3–4, 6, 29, 33, 38, 46–47, 51–52
UFO 66
victimhood 28, 58, 71, 76
violence 19, 39
war 1, 20, 35

About the author:

Roland Kriewaldt is a German-born Canadian author and musician residing near Toronto, Canada. Aside from writing books on human psychology, he has also spent years touring the US and Canada with live bands and working in the graphic and web design field. In his spare time he tries to make life easier for wild animals.

Upcoming books by Roland Kriewaldt:
www.AuroraSkyPublishing.com

Roland's personal website:
www.RolandK.ca

BOOKS:
Clearing a Path to Joy (And finding contentment along the way) — a book to help you navigate the obstacles to joy, from your own self-defeating thoughts to the conflicting agendas of your parents, culture or leaders.

Reality Checks for Everyday Life — A book of "loaded questions" to enlighten and entertain the thinking class.

MUSIC:
Too Big To Fail — Music & Info-Motion Video Project
(Written and performed by Roland Kriewaldt).
(More info: www.music.Rolandk.ca)

OTHER PROJECTS:
Citizen-Based Social Planning.
(More info: www.cbsp.Rolandk.ca)

Notes:

www.ingramcontent.com/pod-product-compliance
Lightning Source LLC
Chambersburg PA
CBHW031427290426
44110CB00011B/564